The Writer

To Chris

Best wishes

Mary Earle.

This book is dedicated to all the scribes
of Mokas Writing Group
who have inspired me.
And in memory of
Julie and Steve who are
sadly missed.
Thank you all so very much

The Writer

Creative, emotive short stories for women
Sit back, relax and be enthralled

Mary E Earle

RAINBOWS END

First published in the United Kingdom in 2010
by Rainbows End

ISBN 978-0-9567264-0-7

Edited by Fiona Thornton
Produced by the Choir Press

Contents

Take a journey with me as I explore my experiences as a member of a writing group. It's the journey of someone who, at first, found the literary world totally alien to her.

From the first fearful steps that were taken into this unknown world of creative writing to tears, frustrations, laughter and joy of the finally completed manuscript.

Read about the challenges that I overcame to create stories, compose poems and pen monologues.

My personal journey is openly described, pulling together the contents for the book and giving it a real feel-good factor.

Inspirational stories, thought provoking experiences, endearing moments, human drama, poignant explosive memories and quirky rhyme to poetic line all make this book a colourful template to capture the imagination.

Introduction

It was with fear and trepidation that I found myself walking towards Mokas Coffee Shop in Cheltenham. I'd read an advertisement for a writers' group. Mmm, that sounds interesting, I thought. Perhaps I will give it a whirl.

What is a writers' group? You may well ask. I had no idea what went on in a writers' group, other than of course writing.

So here I was: notebook at the ready, various pencils and pens clutched tightly in my hand, although I don't think I could have written anything as my hand shook so much.

Come on Mary, no one's going to eat you, they'll just be a bunch of people from all walks of life who want to express their creativity on paper. Self doubt is an amazing thing: it can grip you like a pair of crab-like pincers and before you know it your feet want to walk backwards and disappear down the nearest side street back to the car.

No, stick to the plan girl. Ah, there it is, and I stood and looked at the coffee shop perched on the corner of Suffolk Parade. Blimey – lots of people in there too, perhaps they're full and I've missed my chance. No, come on, Liggy who is running the group had sounded really nice when I had telephoned her, so she knew I was coming.

Before I knew it the door had clanged open and there I was in the steamy interior of the coffee shop listening to the babble of voices as people mingled and made general conversation.

This was going to be interesting as we all sat around a long table and were to introduce ourselves, say why we wanted to join a writers' group and what we expected to get from it.

Well, as each person spoke about his or her creative history my heart began to sink. Screenplays – what! I thought we were just going to be doing a bit of scribbling. Novels already sent to publishers, albeit not accepted as yet. Short stories, long stories, epilogues, monologues, prose – for goodness' sake! I felt I was sinking. I never was a good swimmer anyway. Perhaps I should have brought a life-belt with me, or at least some arm-bands.

I never knew there were so many books on the market and that people could quote the titles, authors, dates of publication etc; boy was I living in a different world for sure.

Actors and actresses graced the table along with would-be writers: a rich colourful group of people we definitely were.

Oh my word, it's nearly my turn. Oh no – it's my turn. And as all eyes focused on me, my stomach somersaulted, my mouth went dry and a tiny voice squeaked out.

Umm, well … I'm Mary Earle and I … I … I … want to write. Of course I bloody well do or I wouldn't be at a writers' group for goodness' sake. Deep breath girl, that's it, just steady yourself. And all of a sudden my voice became loud and clear as I explained that I had done a little writing when I was younger and would like to start again but needed some encouragement and motivation to get me launched. Phew, that wasn't too bad. No one laughed or fled the room. I'd done it; I'd begun the journey of 'The Writer'.

The Beginning

Well I have come back, and this is serious stuff, down to the writing business now – or so I thought. Actually I was a little disappointed at the next meeting, as we didn't get to drag our pens or pencils across scraps of paper and hope that by some magic, words would assemble themselves into some exciting readable script. OK so we formulated the group, its purpose and how to go forward. Hooray too, not so many people were there (selfish ole me) and I felt less intimidated.

I nearly peed my knickers when there was a discussion about styles. Styles? What? I thought this was about writing not hairdressing. What's a style for heaven's sake? Don't panic my love just wait and see what others say, bluff it out. And so I did. It is surprising what you can get away with if you just wait; someone always seems to know everything and I learnt a lot very quietly and could then pitch my bit in without the embarrassment of being seen to be uneducated about writing terminology.

Ha ha! We are going to do the deed next time, it is agreed, and my long fingers curled around my pen letting it know that soon the action would start and the next bestseller would flow from the inky tip of my cheap biro. I retracted the insult to my pen very quickly. After all this is the tool that would lead me to fame, stardom and who knows – the acclaimed mention or appearance on the *Richard & Judy* show. Bring it on down.

Next Time

This is it, this is really, really it. We are gathered here together (no it's not a sermon) to begin, start, launch ourselves into the literary world. Perhaps I'll get to meet J.K.; after all she wrote good old HP in a café, so why can't I follow in her footsteps?

A theme of indecision was the order of the day, and being given a short passage along these lines, the bombshell was dropped.

'Right then,' said Liggy. 'We'll write for the next forty-five minutes but after ten I will give you a curve ball.'

A what? Curve ball! I didn't know this had anything to do with baseball. Very meekly I asked, 'What's a curve ball, miss?' Oh gawd I've regressed back to childhood, like I was sitting in the schoolroom asking the teacher shyly for an explanation. So she explained, very explicit she was our Liggy.

'After ten minutes I will name an object and you have to incorporate it into your story at that precise point.'

Oh come on, how the hell can you do that? I felt like I'd been thrown into a wild sea, and was thrashing around trying to keep my head above water. I was caught in the fear. Right, Mary. Visualise yourself on a calm sea, just sailing along, no worries, just allowing the water to hold and support you. So I did – and it worked. My fear of looking a right nincompoop when alas I failed disappeared. Oh happy days.

Pen poised I thought, come on girl, let some unseen force take over. I believe there is an angel for everything and there just had to be one available this minute to help with my writing. It was amazing. A flow of energy seemed to enter my body and rush into my hand and my pen began to dash across the page. Word after word appeared and when the first curve ball was given it fitted perfectly into my story. Words became sentences, the sentences turned into paragraphs and dots and commas plonked themselves in the most appropriate places. By the time I had finished I was shaking. Oh my word what was that all about?

So here is the first short story in all its glory that my fair hand has ever penned. Creativity has flowed, courage has ensued and confidence has grown. Oh, and if you're curious, the curve balls are in italics.

Justice Needed to be Done

Indecision, well, what the hell! Wondering, puzzling, questioning trying to find a way to come to some conclusion. Turmoil she had never, ever experienced before flowed through her like an electrical force. Aagh ... Will the decision ever come and will it be the right one to have made? Help. Restless, agitated, pacing up and down, weighing all things up, trying to visualise how the decision will unfold the next chapter of her life. She knew once it had been made there would be no turning back. No chance to change her mind. The deed will have been done.

For years there had been this dilemma and it had driven her crazy. Yet she put on her mask, whether it was the happy one, the terrified one, the smiley one, the miserable one or the one of laughter that sometimes nearly took her to hysterical tears. There was such a fine dividing line between them.

She gazed out of the window and felt her heart beating loudly; it seemed to pound in her ears as she thought of the agony of finally making her decision.

As she stared out into the dark night her attention was

drawn to the thousands of stars twinkling, shimmering and shining high in the heavens. Her world had felt so heavenly until that fateful day. How can you be so ecstatically happy and then your world seem to crash around you? Joy, happiness and peace of mind seemed to have been sucked down into some muddy whirling vortex and terror had taken its place, like a dark cloak wrapping itself around her, and all sense of normality had slipped silently away.

A dog barked in the distance and she felt herself transported back in time to that day, such a beautiful happy day that had been spent at their cottage on the beach.

She remembered the soft touch of his fingertips as he slowly stroked her cheek and the feel of velvet lips touching hers. The excitement of it had sent shivers cascading through her body. He had teased and nibbled his way around her body with such loving playfulness, fumbling with her clothes, tugging and pulling at them to enable him to make contact with her silky bare skin. Their passion eventually overwhelmed them and they had stripped each other's clothes off in eager anticipation. He seductively traced his warm tongue over her then naked body, and when his hot breath had reached just below her navel, well. Like the wind whirling around a mountain peak, swirling, twisting until they felt weightless and flew free, their ecstasy peaked and their damp bodies slumped onto the bed while their gasping breath calmed and exhaustion took over. They slept, their naked bodies bathed by the gentle warmth of the now fading afternoon sun. Her body quivered as she allowed herself to be immersed in those poignant memories. The loving, the kindness the tenderness had been just magical. She'd felt she'd found heaven, her soul mate to journey with through life. However it now sometimes felt as though it hadn't happened to her, but that it had happened to someone else a long, long time ago.

Decisions; decisions; decisions, how she hated that word. It seemed to echo round her head, spin out and ricochet off the walls and back to her, to be fully locked inside her head once more.

She shivered as the chill wind that blew from the moors raced inside the open window and placed its icy fingers around her body. Slamming the window shut she dragged the heavy drapes across and obliterated the night.

Somehow she still felt she was in the dark as she walked slowly over to the bedside table and picking up the *diary*, held it in her hands. A great sadness overwhelmed her and the tears streamed unrelenting from her eyes and splashed onto its velvet cover. Shaking, she slowly opened the diary and flicking through the well-worn pages to the tenth of December once more read the words that had become etched in her mind. Why, oh why did she have to find this damn diary, why couldn't it have lain hidden forever more? What had made her pull that drawer out of the old desk that had lain dusty and unused for so many years in the attic? If in that moment she had just turned away she would not have had this terrible, heart-wrenching dilemma. Decisions; indecision like a ping-pong ball being batted back and forth, back and forth. But no, it was a hopeless situation and there really had been no choice.

Fear gripped her once more, her mouth became dry and her legs felt weak. All became a little blurred and she had to sit down on the bed or she would have fallen onto the floor in a quivering heap.

She began to pray: not something she ever really did but somehow it shifted her thoughts to something else. Wondering if her prayers would ever be heard she felt a warmth start to envelop her. At first she thought it was her imagination, but slowly she began to realise that there was a beautiful feeling taking her over, and it came as an *incredible surprise*. Maybe there was something in this praying thing after all. She stretched herself, got up and walked slowly back to the window. Reaching up she pulled the drapes open again and as they creaked and groaned on their rusty hooks she gazed out once more into the dark night. Her eyes grew wide and her heart beat faster – not with fear of having made her decision but with awesome wonder at the sight that was there below her on the drive.

His silhouetted figure stood there and he looked up, she could sense the malice in his eyes. But she knew his arrogance would keep him in a place of false security.

'GET REAL,' she said loudly.

She never did like that drive. What she had planned had been overruled and yet again she had given in. That was a mistake she knew now. There had been times when she'd sat and wept alone in the summerhouse chastising herself for not standing up to him. But it wasn't that easy. If she had stood her ground she knew her life would have been hell, more hellish than it already was.

Gently she touched her arms where some of the scars were still etched into her tender pale skin. Respectable, outstanding pillar of the community she heard people say. They had no idea, no idea whatsoever of how this person was behind his front door. She shook as she looked again at the sight below her. She marvelled at what was happening. For so long she had longed to see this very thing unfolding before her eyes.

And, now no longer afraid, she left the bedroom which had been her sanctuary on so many occasions. Head held high and her back straight, she took a deep breath and stepping onto the landing walked purposefully to face what she knew was the outcome of her decision.

She stumbled a little and grabbed the banister rail to steady herself. Her heart missed a beat. But, taking a deep breath, she began her descent down the sweeping staircase. She gave a start as the bottom treads creaked and groaned under her weight. He never had got them repaired, but that was him all over.

'Leave them to me,' he would quip.

But she knew there were always more important things for him to do, which of course would benefit him. He was always out there doing 'good' in the local area. Well, the community, his, as he referred to it, was going to have an enormous shock. She described his ego once to some friends as being 'as big as the Empire State Building, and needing to be constantly fed'.

Well now he was getting a real wake-up call and one he couldn't squirm out of. She choked the words out, 'The rat!' The anger was beginning to well up inside her, building until her body shook from the intensity of it. Deep sighs escaped her tense body, her cheeks felt hot, and perspiration could be felt on areas of her skin. There was just one more thing she needed to do, the thing she'd always done when she felt hopeless and helpless and anger engulfed her. However this time it would be different, she was no longer helpless and it was no longer a *hopeless situation*, things were drastically about to change.

Walking into her study she locked the door. Good, the drapes had been pulled over before Janet the maid had left for her evening off. Making her way to her desk she fumbled for the key she kept in her handbag. Ah, there it was, clipped inside the lining as usual. He'd never dared to force the drawer open; for sure she would have known it was him. The key turned easily and there was that heightened sense of anticipation she felt every time she opened it.

Now, there it was, the knife, the swabs. Taking the blade she made her way to her usual chair; it was a welcome friend, somehow its familiarity comforted her. Settling into the soft cushions she rolled up her sleeve and, having swabbed her arm, drew the knife across her skin. Never too deep; just enough pressure. Ah, she could feel the tension in her body lessening, the anger subsiding as the blood trickled slowly from the fresh cut. It always eased her feelings, always brought relief. The therapist she'd been secretly seeing had really helped her understand why she behaved in this way. This was to be the last time. Never again. Life was going to be different from now on, very different.

In the past she'd contemplated cutting her wrists but she'd never wanted to give him the satisfaction. For years she'd thought of ways of getting her own back. Now it was happening. Justice needed to be done!

She walked slowly to the kitchen taking the no longer needed items with her, parcelled them securely and safely, then dropped them into the rubbish bin. There, done and dusted, and she felt great.

There was a resounding knock on the front door that jarred her back to the matter in hand. She knew she was now ready to face the world. With a smile on her face she walked out into the hallway and checked her appearance in the long ornate mirror. Her shoulder-length blonde hair looked immaculate pinned high on her head with a few wispy tendrils falling against her beautifully made-up face. As usual nothing was out of place. Keeping up appearances he had called it, and so the game goes on, although now she felt there was nothing wrong in it. It was her choice to continue to look well turned-out, in fact she felt a little smug about it. Then with a satisfied look on her face she clasped the doorknob and threw the door open.

'Good evening, Mrs Hutchinson, are you all right?'

'Yes, thank you,' she replied calmly, 'I'm ready now, shall we go?'

It had all been carefully planned. Eighteen months ago

she'd redecorated the lounge and he'd never known about the minuscule cameras that had been hidden. It had been well worth the money, and it certainly hadn't come cheap. Fortunately her mother had paid the account for her so he wouldn't become suspicious. She had out-smarted him and that had giving her a feeling of power. The secret was out and soon everyone would know when it hit the headlines in the press. She could picture it now and it thrilled her.

'About time too,' she thought.

She'd been given such good advice when at last she had sought help, and now, at long last, it was over. Her GP had meticulously recorded her every visit, carefully noting any mark on her body resulting from the abusive behaviour of her husband. Her logbook had been filled in with every detail of any incident, however small. Everything was penned clearly, nothing was left out.

The day she opened up to a dear trusted friend and showed her her back covered in cigarette burns had been the turning point in her life. Yes, the scars would remain but now she felt she had her dignity back, some control. She was no longer powerless.

The car with its blue flashing lights had now disappeared from view. The relief was amazing: she was free. The nightmare was over and she had an inner strength she'd never experienced before and along with all the support that was now in place she would be able to deal with the next stage.

As she climbed into the back of the police car the warm hand of the woman police officer she'd come to know over the past months kindly touched her arm.

'Don't worry, the evidence is so strong Mrs Hutchinson, you've been very brave. Some women can never do what you have done you know. Yes, you've been very courageous.'

And as they sped away she knew the nightmare was over, a new life lay before her and she was at last free. She pictured in her mind the large bold letters of the 'breaking news'. LOCAL DIGNITARY BEATS WIFE. Overwhelming evidence could lead to the conviction of popular, pillar of the community Richard James Hutchinson. Documented reports have been made, and supported by diary entries of his illicit affair with international playboy Kevin Peter Richardson.

She smiled, and with her right hand removed her wedding ring. The now open car window allowed the cool night air to rush in and with a triumphant thrust she threw the ring out into the darkness.

So the journey continues, and each week there is a fear that nothing will happen. That my pen will stay grasped in my fingers and not even twitch. Oh fear, how I hate you. Please don't get in the way of the creative force that can flow through me. Please don't block the energy that can be released. Let me write, put pen to paper, formulate, dash off. Please, please, please …

Then it came, a rush of energy that took me over, and although it wasn't so powerful and I wasn't shaking any more, the stories still kept coming.

Hip, hip hooray, I am a very happy woman and so proud of myself.

Freezing

The child, his face flushed red from the icy wind, bent and picked the stone from the hard, frozen ground.

His hat pulled down tightly over his ears at least created some barrier from the biting cold.

Small fingers, now tightly curled around the hard rock, began to tingle; there was no escaping the frosty air. It seemed to penetrate every part of his body. 'Brrrrrrr,' and he gave himself a shake.

Pausing, he let his mind wander along numerous pathways in his head, but all led to the same place. Is this really happening?

With a quick thrust his arm threw the rock and as the anger raced from his now numbed fingers he hurled it with force into the air. His breathing was laboured and white vapour trails reached out in front of him. The rock hit the ice with a resounding crash and like a pane of glass it shattered in every direction. The rock fell deep into the murky depths of the water.

His breathing eased and he rammed his hands into his coat pockets and studied the hole where his ammunition had broken through the sheet of ice. It was jagged and there were cracks running off in all directions, but in the middle sat the gaping hole where the cold water still rippled. The edges of the ice looked as though they could easily slice through flesh. He shivered.

He wondered whether the broken shards had fallen down into the water with the rock or would they have melted, being away from the freezing surface? After all it was only the top layer that had frozen. Looking hard he could see some of the pieces floating, gently bobbing on the top of the exposed water.

A lopsided grin appeared across his young face. I don't suppose it matters anyway, does it? Things come and go, change, re-form and sometimes disappear into oblivion. I wonder if that's what my mates will think about me? Perhaps they'll think that I don't exist any more.

Life's a strange thing he decided. Yesterday he was happily riding his bike with his mates around the park, their laughter ringing out across the empty space. No one seemed to venture out in this bitter weather. But they had. They'd bought hot-dogs and crammed them into hungry mouths, the steam visible as they'd munched and chewed their way through the deliciously hot food. Boy they were just yummy.

The gurgling in his stomach caught his attention. He gave it a prod and told it to shut up; there were several more resounding gurgles before there was silence. Here he was in isolation, pondering life. Well, why not? Wasn't it rather heavy for a lad of ten to be questioning life? Perhaps, perhaps not.

Drawing his eyes back to the sheet of ice, which stretched out before him, he let his imagination run wild.

The skates, which were fixed firmly to his feet, slid easily on the pond's surface and cut through its crusty top leaving a trail of ice particles in his wake. Gracefully like a swan he glided, turned, spun, pirouetted and then to the roar of rapturous applause performed an intricate jump that brought oohs and aahs from the audience.

The sound of a crow startled him and he realised his feet were freezing. His arms and legs began to move involuntarily and before he knew it he was frantically star jumping. In out, in out, breathing hard and fast, puffs of white breath billowing out of his cold lips. In out, in out he chanted as he jumped, encouraging the blood to race faster in his body, his young legs moving faster and faster until he gasped for breath and the cold air clutched at the back of his throat making it ache.

'Robin, Robin.' A voice loud and clear floated across the field. 'Robin, what are you doing? Come on, it's time to go!'

The young mind kicked into gear. A burst of excitement and fear shot through him. All traces of anger gone now. He opened his mouth wide, cupped his now warmed hands around his lips and yelled, 'OK, Dad, I'm coming.'

Glancing around he absorbed greedily into his memory bank all that he could see before him. The frozen pond, the tree with snow-white frost clinging to its branches, the mist that was slowly receding over the fields and allowing the forms of sheep to appear, the coal-black crows that were such a contrast to the white frost. Hmm, don't let me ever forget this wintry scene. But of course he would.

I guess all the memories will be eventually replaced by new ones and then all I knew will fade into the background. He so much wanted to keep it all alive and take everything with him. A deep sigh escaped his young body and his breath, fluffy and white, flowed into the freezing air.

'Robin, come on!' His father's voice sounded agitated now.

'Coming,' he replied. And his feet flew across the grass as he raced over to the front gate that had now been closed for the last time by his dad.

'Come on lad, we've a long journey ahead of us.'

Without hesitation Robin jumped into the back of the car, and as it drew away the SOLD sign seemed to wink at him.

He laughed and turned to his mum and said, 'I wonder what Australia's like?'

'A darn sight warmer than here,' she replied.

'Yeah, it'll be a darn sight warmer for sure,' and Robin's excited chatter kept them all amused as they sped off to the airport.

So what is the task tonight? What will inspire me? Will again the writer produce a masterpiece? Or will a damp squib lie before me as my scribbles fail to make sense? With shame I would look at the group and nervously explain, 'Nothing ... nothing came, just blank.'

The music played. A lilting, melodious piece that should trigger our creative self and inspire us all to write and write and write.

Oh, here it comes. Deliciously exciting, as word after word formed and slid easily onto the page.

Haunting Melody

There was a hushed silence and the sounds of the orchestra receded before the cacophony of Imelda's cue struck up.

She stood poised in the wings, breathing deeply to compose herself and feeling the thrill and excitement coursing through her trim body. Her dress, the deepest shade of turquoise and made of net and silk, fell neatly into its many folds and the bodice encrusted with jewels held her pert breasts firmly.

Then without hesitation she was moving with elegance onto the stage. Sure and graceful as always, the haunting floating violins filling the auditorium as though the sounds embraced everyone that sat there with concentrated anticipation.

From the audience there were gasps of delight as she pirouetted around on the stage, her dress flowing out and revealing her trim, strong legs elegantly clad in the sheerest of tights. The other dancers swirling, moving gently and surely, started to melt into the background, slowly fading out of sight as the spotlight continued to follow Imelda on her journey around the stage.

There stood Petrya, standing poised, body firm, muscles hard and taut beneath his shimmering leotard. She could see his manliness bulging where the tops of his legs met. She brought herself back to her dance as gracefully she moved with slow sureness towards him, and the spotlights whirled around them as they clasped each other's hands and stared into each other's eyes with longing as secret lovers often did.

You could feel the tension in the audience as expectantly they watched, riveted to the two lovers as they warmly embraced each other. Their lithe vibrant bodies seem to become as one, as with amazing grace they moved around the stage with the passion each of them felt.

The music rose and swelled like a stormy sea, as if waves were building in height and crashing onto the shore with a roar. Their passion and agony were so visible and always there were gasps from the audience as the two lovers melted once more into each other's arms and kissed.

They sprang apart and Petrya looking with downcast eyes and then with agonising movements touched Imelda on her cheek and danced with a ravaged look of pain on his face away into the trees and disappeared into the darkness.

Imelda's dance that followed portrayed the wretchedness she felt and tears sprang from the eyes of some of those watching who were captivated by the agony and pain of this young, beautiful girl separated from her lover.

She came back to reality with a start as raindrops fell from a bleak, grey, cloudy sky onto her head, face and neck. Like cold icy fingers touching her and sending shivers through her already freezing body, the rain continued endlessly in its torturous descent.

Standing on the narrow stone bridge she felt a million miles away from the times when they had danced together around the world. It was always the same, the gasps from the audience, the tears, the rapturous applause, and the flowers. She could almost smell them now. The adulation, the excitement and then returning to the privacy of their hotel room. They still had enough energy to fall into each other's arms and let their passion rise and fall, each touch of their bodies like an electric shock coursing through them as they reached that place of ecstasy and lay exhausted, drifting off into a deep, deep, dreamless sleep entwined in each other's arms.

She came back once more to the cold, dark night as underneath the bridge raced the river, bursting its banks from days of winter storms. It was a desolate place, as was her heart. All around the wildness of the moors, and the distant hills rising like monsters waiting to march in and eat her up.

Ten years ago she was Imelda, elegant, young and so in love. They had lived for each other and danced for each other, never tiring of each other's company, that excitement always there, and when they eventually married they had been ecstatically happy for so long with the richness of their love.

Then five years ago on the way home from the theatre in Moscow a group of drunken youths, clutching vodka bottles, had shattered their world. She remembered their performance that evening had felt different: as though they had danced with an even greater passion and agony almost as though never again would they grace the stages of the world with their eloquent movements and vibrant passion.

The youths had set on Petrya for no reason. Their laughter would haunt her in her sleep, when she could sleep. Even the sleeping tablets the doctor prescribed didn't seem to have any effect. The sickly smiles of those crazed boys seemed to peer at her out of everything, even the trees and flowers. Wherever she went they came to torment her. They had egged each other on, ceaselessly grinning, laughing and shouting. Then that terrible silence had descended and they had scattered into the night while her screams echoed round and round the dark alleyways among the drab, grey buildings.

She remembered looking down and Petrya's beaten, broken body lay limp in a pool of sickly sweet blood which was still spilling from the knife wound in his chest.

No more could she live with the torment. She wasn't Imelda any more but a shell of her. Her fat body covered in old drab clothes all felt so alien to her. Not a spark of her former self was left.

Somehow she had got through those long dark days and nights that followed. But now enough was enough. She climbed onto the wall of the bridge, struggling to stand upright in the wild wind that battered her, and looked down into the whirling waters. As she stepped forward into the abyss Petrya's smiling face came to greet her and she felt his arms once more around her as she fell into the roaring, raging water and they were carried away together.

She felt no pain, as peace descended on her and as she took her last gasping breath her body went limp.

The old fisherman who was strolling home that night never did understand or make sense of what he saw, as two balls of golden, shining light rose shimmering from the tumbling, rushing water up into the stormy night sky. A haunting melody seemed to swirl around him, almost as if hundreds of bows gently skimmed the strings of violins. Maybe it was those two extra drams of whisky he had downed at the Stag's Head, who knows. 'Best keep it to meself,' he had thought as he staggered on into the wild, windy night scratching his cold, wet head.

The Monologue Challenge

We were sat very happily in the pub snug, a venue we used if our leader Liggy was away and the coffee shop was closed to the group. My heart turned a somersault when I heard the objective for the evening.

'Right,' thus spoke the delegated leader for that night. 'Right, tonight is monologue night!'

Like hell it is, my mind replied. Shit. What's a monologue? Is anyone asking, questioning. No. They're all nodding their heads.

'That's fun,' they echoed. 'Oh goody.'

Clever clogs the lot of them, know-it-alls. These were the words that reverberated in my head. Bet they're crap at it!

'Shut up, Mary,' my inner voice shouted, 'don't be so negative. Rise to the challenge.'

'Peter,' I heard myself saying. 'Actually what is a monologue, I'm not really sure?'

'Well, the easiest way to describe it is a long speech by one person that is usually humorous.'

Voices chipped in. 'You know Joyce Grenfell. She was really famous for her monologues. You must have heard some of them, especially the one about the school children: "George don't do that!".'

'Oh yes, of course,' I replied.

The words I'd heard earlier in my head repeated themselves. Load of clever clogs. That's what they are. Bloody know-it-alls.

So with a smile on my face and a look of knowingness beaming from me I set to work.

The trials and tribulations of a writer fresh on the scene.

Successful? Or a has-been?!

A poem, phrase or couplet
Adorn a page or two
But what the hell's a monologue?
I don't know what to do!

No one told me I'd have
To write this stuff
Should have gone to painting
And messed with a brush

My head's gone all fuzzy
As brain tries to think
Oh stuff these monologues
They just stink!

***

Cluttered mind
Empty head
Where's the words?
Fear and dread

What's the title?
Next words for the line
Oh for gawd's sake
I'm out of time

Something's filtering
Brain's a-twitch
Scratch my head
It's just an itch!

Now it's coming
Quick and clear
Words are pouring
Look my dear

It's quite quirky
Humourous too
Wow I've written –
Well done you!

Mary E Earle

It's a Fair Cop

I went to a dinner party the other day,
My daughter's future in-laws had come to stay.
Needing to make a good impression
I racked my brains with some discretion.
Remembering an article I'd read about cheese
I related the information with confident ease –
Did you know that in a cheesy ounce
20 million orgasms merrily bounce?
Faces stared back, shocked for sure,
I'd made a gaff, let's go some more.
Can you believe a piece of cheese
Would grab such attention from the attendees?
The laughter began, I knew not why.
Hankies appeared wiping tears from their eyes.
Orgasms? they said from a communal head
20 million orgasms – why you'd be dead!
My stomach churned, my cheeks flushed red
Oh my god, what had I said?
I mean organisms, that's what it was
Oh blimey, crikey, I need help from above
The laughter dried, the tears were mopped
OK, OK, it's a fair cop!

And then I remembered the cake-baking day
For her wedding reception, I say
We stirred and stirred then spooned the mix
With a bottle of brandy we'd had our fix!
The telephone rang – oh no Auntie's dead
The horror we felt has to be said.
Daughter had to drive hastily home
Oh no! Don't leave me all alone!
The cakes were a-cooling

THE WRITER

And I lay a-drooling.
Hey do you know what?
I had tips from the baker's shop
A master-baker told me how
To protect the cakes – wow
Cardboard on top she said
Here it's written down, so I duly read
How helped the master-baker that day
Got to say it, yes hooray.

It was deathly silent, not a breath
A master-baker I repeated with dread.
Flailing their hands to left and right
A chorus of laughter filled the night
Couldn't tell what they were thinking
Looks could kill, I went on speaking.
For Christ's sake you lot, what are you doing?
Chuckling, laughing, fro-ing and to-ing
Master-baker, master-baker bounced in my head
For god's sake, I want to be dead
My blushes were bright
Yet another sticky plight
That's it, I'm going
God bless you – goodnight!

Mary E Earle

Paint Brush

Paint brush at the ready
Here we go, keep it steady.
Damn it's dripped on carpet – phew!
Stupid fool! What shall I do?
Clutching cloth soaked in turps
Rubbing hard for all I'm worth.
Ah, that's it; all is clean
Back to painting, see it gleam.

Oh my gawd! A great big hair
Has fixed itself, I just stare.
How I pick at sticky paint
Hair is staying, no you ain't!
What to do, I'm in a mood.
Just keep calm, get some food.
Hair now gone, it's left a streak.
Perhaps it will go by next week.

Stamp my foot, huff and puff,
This painting lark looks pretty rough.
Cursing, swearing, I kick the tin.
Head is now in mighty spin.
Face appears with cheesy grin.
What's up my love, I heard a row
You've spilt the paint, you silly cow.
Carpet new, we'll have to get.
I'll come with you I need to vet.

Later in a nice warm bath
I chuckle, sigh with happy laugh.
The only way I'd get my way
The only way that he would pay.

THE WRITER

Was if he thought it was a fluke
That paint was spilled by my boot!

My plan had worked
The act was done
New carpet now – I had won!

***

No, no it can't be such a task.
Heart beating very fast,
Hands just shook.
Write a story for a book.
A story, at least 6,000 words.
Oh come off it, you're just nerds.
What do you mean?
It's true alas
My creativity I'll now trash
It cannot be, I cannot see

How possibly I can agree
To write this piece of epic length
I've gone so weak I have no strength
But here I go – something's forming
Oh happy days, inspiration's dawning.

Old Tom

The finger, its flesh old and wrinkled, touched the steamed-up window and traced a crooked line through the misty film.

Inside old Tom's head a million thoughts rushed backwards and forwards until they became a tangled mess. His head hung low on his shoulders now, a forlorn expression spread across his face. He'd often slip away into this place of darkness and despair, the sounds of the busy coffee shop happening all around him, but the staff and customers were oblivious to this tired old man.

What's life been all about? he pondered. It doesn't really make any sense to me at all. It all feels so pointless, so futile.

He coughed loudly, his chest rasping as he caught his breath and gasped for air. Then silence resumed until a sigh escaped from his toilworn body. Peace, that's what I want, peace. Every night I pray the Lord will take me but there I am every morning opening my eyes and straining to see if I've moved to that place called heaven. But no, those dull grey walls close in on me and the cobwebs are still hanging in the corners. Even they're covered in dust, their eight-legged inmates long gone.

He added more streaks to the moisture, which was now

dribbling slowly down the glass. He muttered aloud, his voice a garbled mess, like the thoughts in his head. Just waiting for it all to be over, that's what it feels like, waiting for the end.

Tom was now in his late eighties, in fact, after thinking hard he realised he was nearly ninety. He had now reverted to using a walking stick, not one of them fancy fold-up things mind you, but an old one that had been cut from the hedgerow. It was bent and gnarled like his body. In fact they made good friends, having things in common like. He loved running his fingers over the smooth ridges; somehow it soothed him. How on earth could you tell someone you felt comforted by your walking stick?

Amazingly he had kept his head of unruly, curly, brown hair. He didn't brush it much, and when it became too long he'd pick up the old kitchen scissors, drag their blunted edges through the handful of hair he'd bunched up, and chomp it off! The old greasy cap that he wore hid it nicely. After all he could always push the straggly bits up underneath to keep it somewhat tidy.

He'd always had a twinkle in his eyes, yet it belied how he was feeling deep inside. If someone had opened him up and taken a look at his heart they would have found deep, red slashes across it, and tiny arrows deeply embedded.

Although he wasn't fastidious about his appearance so much now he did manage to get to the launderette now and then. Betty Parsons who managed the launderette was a right character and she used to have Tom 'laughing his socks off' when she'd recounted her escapades as a young girl. She was a right one that Betty by all accounts. He thought of the machines whirling, clicking and spinning. It quite amused him to sit and watch the acrobatic tumbling of the clothes as they swirled and spun through their cycles.

Somewhat like life really. The swirling of thoughts in his mind, how they tumbled around and made little sense, then spun out somewhere into the ether to be borne away by the wind or washed away by the rain.

His finger felt cold now so he stopped its movements across the glass and opened his eyes to look at the maze of lines he'd etched through the steam. Tracks of my years, he thought, and there have been many of them. Roads to here and there, and roads to nowhere.

Pulling his scarf around his neck he called to Bonnie to bring him another mug of the strong tea he always liked to drink. 'I think I'll have one of those dripping cakes too,' he shouted. 'I feel a bit peckish come to think of it.'

'All right Tom. I'll be over in a minute,' Bonnie replied, a sing-song sound to her voice.

Tom scratched his stubbly chin. Shaving wasn't one of his favourite tasks. In fact he found it more of a chore lately. Then, recently everything seemed to be taking more effort.

'There you are Tom,' and Bonnie placed the steaming mug of tea in front of him along with a dripping cake, much his favourite.

'Thanks love. You know I remember when I was a lad and had to go to the bakers for **him**, I mean father, first thing in the morning. They were fresh out of the oven when I went, sitting there on the hot oven tray stuffed full of currants with a thick toffee layer on the base. I can hear the baker's voice now, "What you doing here lad? I ain't open yet."

'I'd start to walk away and he would call out, "Where you off to then? Come back here." I never gave him any backchat and the baker would reward me by slipping an extra drip as he called them into the bag. But I never ate it. I always shared it among the family when I got home. I can smell them now,' and Tom licked his lips and smiled.

Bonnie patted Tom on the shoulder and left him to his

reverie. She knew that he liked to sit and ponder. But she couldn't help feeling concerned for old Tom; she felt he had experienced a rough passage through life.

Munching his drip and drinking down the tea gave Tom something different to think about other than his maudlin reminiscences. He started counting the currants, and they could be easily counted. Today's drips certainly weren't like the ones he had enjoyed in his youth.

He shifted on his seat, his sciatica was playing him up something chronic, but then at nearly ninety you expected a twinge or two. It didn't really help that his flat was damp and he wasn't always very particular about having well-aired bedclothes.

Bonnie glanced over at him and smiled. She noticed his jumper had more holes in it and that there were odd laces in his old brogues. The cigarette ash had left a trail down the front of his jumper and the front of his baggy trousers looked, well perhaps it's best not to think too much about those.

Abigail, the other waitress, sidled up to Bonnie and shiftily glanced at Tom. 'I wish he wouldn't sit in the window, not a good advertisement for Mokas is it? Enough to put anyone off, seeing a bedraggled old man sitting there.'

'Oh don't be so horrible Abigail,' Bonnie threw at her. 'He's harmless enough, just a bit lonely and he isn't hurting anyone, is he?'

'Well I don't like him,' and Abigail went off huffing and puffing to clear the tables of the dirty dishes left behind by the fast disappearing customers.

Bonnie stared her straight in the face, 'Just don't you dare say it. You know it's the end of the afternoon rush,' and she went back to making the sandwiches ready for tomorrow's hungry customers.

Abigail was in a right mood and a scowl broke across her

young face. Suddenly a glass slid clumsily from her well-manicured fingers and with a crash shattered into minute pieces on the floor.

Tom jerked back in his seat and then his eyes glazed over, his mind whirling as he was transported back in time. Sucked uncontrollably by a long, dark, revolving tunnel. He had no control over it, it enveloped him, consumed him in every sense.

Bang, crash. Shells exploded all around him. The sound of bullets could be heard ricocheting off tin helmets, sometimes followed by groans and cries for help. Mud and bits of bodies splattered him as he struggled to right himself in the wet stinking trench.

Bodies huddled together, some wounded, and blood oozing from freshly ripped and jagged flesh. Others crying, crying for their loved ones or even their mothers as they struggled to draw breath into their exhausted, emaciated bodies. The stench would fill his nostrils, a retching feeling would start in his stomach. At times he would have to cover his eyes from the terrible sights that were there right before him. No one should have to bear witness to the horrors that were so much a part of war.

Tom remembered a young boy called Simon looking at him, his eyes wide, and a shocked look on his face.

'Eh son, come on, you'll be just fine,' Tom's voice sounded none too reassuring. 'This bloody war's going to end soon. It has to.'

'Sarge you've been saying that every day for four months and it's always the same. There's no let up is there? It never stops. I'm scared sarge, real scared.' He went to speak again but before the words could force their way past his dry lips, he'd shuddered and a stream of blood bubbled out from his mouth and he fell sideways. There was no sound, just a deathly stillness and wide staring eyes looking out to nowhere.

Tom knew the lad was a gonner and a large, hard lump stuck in his throat. 'I hate this bloody war,' he screamed. He buried his head in his filthy hands and wept, like he'd never wept before.

He was tired of being strong, tired of his men looking to him to cheer them up. Tired of the whole bloody thing called war! 'Why God? Why can't we all live in peace?'

He fumbled in Simon's pockets and drew out a much-crumpled letter. Mud had stained it, and there was damp blood splattered on the cheap beige envelope. On the front were scribbled the words 'Mum and Dad'.

The darkness seemed to engulf him as a huge black cloud gradually descended and seemed to eat him up. Voices in his head wanted to scream out, he felt the pressure increasing as though his skull would crack and his own brains would spill out into the dank, waterlogged trench.

Gradually Tom became aware of someone's voice penetrating into his mind.

'Tom, Tom, come on Tom, it's getting on for closing time and you've still some of your tea to finish.' Bonnie's voice gradually reached through the long dark tunnel he'd slipped into. He came back with a start and stared at his shaking hands. He felt a door closing securely in his mind, he lifted his head and brought his eyes into focus, and realised Bonnie was smiling warmly at him.

'That's it, drink your tea up and I'll walk you home,' her voice light and encouraging.

Tom drank the last of his tea with a gulp, eased himself from the chair and as his joints gradually freed themselves from their inaction staggered to his feet and leant on his old, faithful walking stick. He accidentally nudged the table with his knee, the china rattled noisily, and a knife fell to the floor with a clatter.

Abigail groaned and muttered under her breath, 'Silly old

git,' and went on to begrudgingly clear the table and reluctantly scoop the knife off the floor. 'Banned he ought to be, banned.' And she flounced off with a cocky look on her young, overly made-up face.

'Right then Tom, let's get going, shall we?' And Bonnie followed on behind the doddery old man. 'You lead the way Tom, as I'm not sure where you live. I think you told me once it was a basement flat somewhere in the Suffolks.'

The door of the coffee shop banged behind them. Mokas as it was now named sat on the corner of Suffolk Parade in the area of Cheltenham known as the Suffolks.

Its large picture window looked out onto St James church, which had now been transformed into a pizza restaurant. The smell of garlic, cheese and pepperoni filtered out through the chancel door, the sound of hymn-singing voices a long-distant memory.

The area attracted a large number of winers and diners who spent the evening in jocular social interaction in one of the many restaurants and public houses that graced the area. Large houses rose from the pavements, an assortment of architectural delight which would once have been the scene of upmarket families and attendant servants working hard to keep their owners' respectability and nobility high in society.

No longer could the sound of the clip-clopping of horses' hooves be heard resounding through the streets. Long gone were the piles of hot steaming manure; now the resplendent carriages had been replaced by cars creeping, revving and screeching round tight corners. They filled the air with exhaust fumes for all to breathe, their carbon footprints leaving a mark on this beautiful area of Cheltenham.

Tom leant heavily on his stick now, and paused to draw breath into his labouring lungs. 'Past my best for sure, I am Bonnie. Nearly there now – just down here.'

Rounding yet another corner he stopped before some rusty railings. There was no gate to the steep flight of worn stone steps that took you down to the front door. The paint, obviously once shiny black, was now dull, and peeling away from the wood. Signs of rot were clearly visible in the woodwork.

Turning to Bonnie, a drawn look on his face, he puffed the words out of his dry, cracked lips. 'Thanks, luv, for seeing me home. I'll be fine now.' He swayed a little and placed his brittle, bony fingers on the railings to steady himself.

'No Tom, I'll see you in,' Bonnie stated in no uncertain terms. 'You're not so steady on your pins as you used to be, are you?'

'Whotcha mean? There isn't a darn thing wrong with me my girl. I'm telling you straight, I'm just fine!'

'Why are you stood there swaying then?' Bonnie enquired and she winked at him from her cheery face.

Tom chuckled and winked back, and begrudgingly gave in, 'All right you can see me to my door, but you're not coming in. You understand?'

Bonnie didn't reply and gently steered him down the steps, feeling startled as she felt the skeletal form of his arm beneath her plump hand.

He rummaged for his key in his trousers. There was a piece of string looped to the key and the other end was pinned to the inside of the pocket. 'My mum used to do that when I was a lad. I'm a bit forgetful at times now, so I know exactly where it is and don't have to go rummaging around the flat. I've wasted so much time in the past searching high and low for the darn thing.' He gasped for breath as he came to the end of his long explanation and Bonnie's heart felt heavy.

There was the tunnel again sucking him back, not so dark

but dark enough. He felt dizzy as he whirled down through the years.

'I've told you time and time again Tom, you are not going out to play in the street.' His father's voice resounded around the small parlour resulting in the cups and saucers jingling and jangling on the dresser.

Tom could feel the knot start in the pit of his stomach and his heart started to beat loudly in his small chest.

'I'm not having no lad of mine on the streets,' he shouted. His eyes were bulging and red blotches screamed out from his puffy face as he caught Tom a resounding blow across his young smooth cheek.

Lips wobbling, Tom's eyes welled up. His fists clenched tight, he struggled to hold his arms close to his sides. He'd learnt self-control early in his young life, which had held him in good stead during the war.

His mother sat there, her head bowed. She'd learnt well too not to react. Or the same bullying punishment would be inflicted on her, by this evil, wrathful man.

How Tom hated his father, really hated him. His young body bore the scars and bruises through his childhood, the results of the kicks, thumps, beatings and slaps. Often weals streaked across his flesh, made by the tatty brown belt his father used to strip from his trousers, like a long brown snake wriggling in readiness out from the loops of the waistband.

He remembered the burning marks that scorched his tender skin. The snake would hiss as it wiggled through the air until it found its target and became still.

The brutish punishment was never deserved. Tom learnt early on to be the good boy. To run, fetch and please at every opportunity so he wouldn't be the target for the hissing snake.

The tunnel seemed to draw him deeper and deeper into a

sticky, black substance that took him back to that fateful day. No matter how he tried to claw himself back from the gloop he couldn't free himself.

The scene was unfolding, the pictures he so wanted to escape from became clearer, there was no running away. Would there never be any respite from these dark dismal memories?

His father stood there, his arm raised, the snake in readiness to begin its hissing yet again. There was a putrid look on his face, a snarl on his lips, black dots for eyes and dribble slowly seeping from the corner of his bitter mouth.

'Right you've asked for it lad, you've asked for it and you're going to get it.' His arm rose angrily and as it began to fall, the snake started to hiss. A startled look appeared on his face, the mouth now contorting at a strange angle. 'Aghhhhhhh,' blazed out on his laboured breath as he keeled over and fell with a bang across the only respectable chair they owned. Then crashed, with a resounding thud onto the floor, absolutely still, totally silent, nothing but nothingness.

There was a whooshing sound and Tom felt the pull of life as he once more emerged from the tunnel to find Bonnie's comforting voice steadying him.

He'd realised lately that the padlock he kept securely on his heart and the protective shield he'd surrounded it with was changing. It was almost as if each act of kindness shown to him loosened the padlock and thinned the shield. Once he'd even thought he sensed a tiny glowing golden light shining brightly in his heart. But he'd dismissed it as pure nonsense. However, he could feel a warmth stirring inside as yet again Bonnie's voice unknowingly worked to break down the barriers.

'In a right trance you were Tom. For a minute I felt really

scared,' and Bonnie stared at him out of her big, doleful brown eyes.

'I'm OK, just need a bit of a rest. There, the door's open now, I'll be fine.'

A look of amazement, shock and horror simultaneously crossed Bonnie's face. The putrid smell that had wafted out through the open door seemed to engulf her. She stood there shifting from one foot to the other, not knowing what to say.

Although the hallway was dim she could make out the piles of old newspapers stacked high along the wall. There were black bags scattered around, their contents spilling haphazardly onto the old linoleum-covered floor. Flies buzzed ceaselessly, flitting from rotting, decaying food in the hope of ingesting some delightful morsel to fill their already bloated bodies.

'Tom, oh Tom, I never knew, I never guessed,' and she burst into tears and stood looking at him, a wretched expression spreading across her usually cheerful face. Brushing the tears away, she regained control of her emotions. Taking hold of Tom's arm she pushed him gently along the hallway into what once must have been the sitting room. The same squalor met her and it was all she could do not to retch and rush out into the fresh air.

Tom hung his head, the gnarled fingers working nervously now across the top of his old, faithful stick.

'I never wanted you to find out, luv. I just knew once you realised what a disgusting, wretched person I was you'd have nothing more to do with me. He looked at her, his hazel eyes filled with shame, and two large tears poised ready to begin a slow journey across the wrinkled flesh that formed his cheeks. He took off his cap and passed it backwards and forwards between his hands; his agitation was plain to see. He looked like a naughty little schoolboy who'd been caught out, poised for the punishment he felt would surely come. The thought of the hissing snake made him quiver.

'Nothing to do with you, nothing to do with you, what a load of stuff and nonsense. I care about you Tom, you silly old fool,' and Bonnie gave one of her smiles that always melted his heart.

'I want to help you Tom, yes, help. Now for goodness' sake sit down in that armchair before you keel over,' and Bonnie scooped a large pile of old papers onto the floor to make room for him. 'There you are. Now don't you move, I just need to check out the rest of your flat so I know what I'm dealing with.' She didn't stop to drink in the helpless, pitiful look that had appeared on Tom's face.

Bonnie walked off before he could say a word and stepping over more stinking black bags found herself in what must be the kitchen.

'Oh my word, oh my …,' and her voice trailed off as she surveyed the squalor.

Filthy ashtrays stacked with cigarette butts spilled out onto the grease-layered worktops. Mould grew from little mounds of goodness knows what between black grimy saucepans, dust covered plates and chipped, stained mugs, some with their contents still there with circles of mould floating on the top. She could almost hear the bacteria moving around her, and she was sure there were mouse droppings on the table that was covered in yellowed newspaper. She read the date from the top of one of the pages: 6th August 1970. Her hand shot to her mouth: blimey, that was thirty-seven years ago.

Without daring to open any of the cupboards she backed into the hallway, and walked into the bedroom.

Nothing could have prepared her for the sight that met her eyes, let alone the smell that seeped into her nostrils and grabbed at the back of her throat. The stench of the urine-soaked, flock mattress on the old metal bedstead nearly pushed her over the edge. But she remained long enough to take in the pitiful environment that was Tom's home.

She didn't dare go into the bathroom and the thought of checking out the toilet filled her with horror. So, turning surely and purposefully, Bonnie went and knelt down by Tom's chair and took his old, skinny, fleshy hand in hers and held it lovingly while she spoke.

'Right Tom. This is the plan. No. No buts,' and she put her hand up to silence him. 'Listen carefully. I belong to a wonderful youth group. They're a great bunch of young people. We do all sorts of things for the community and I'm going to ask for volunteers to help sort out your flat. Looks like you haven't been managing too well, have you? So a little help won't go amiss will it? But I need your help with something in return. I want you to come along and talk about some of your experiences in the war to some of the local youngsters. They don't always appreciate what they have in life until they hear how it used to be. You've told me hundreds of amusing snippets since you've been coming into Mokas and I am sure the group would find your stories inspiring. What do you say, is it a deal?'

Tom looked at her and felt the padlock loosen slightly as the warmth from her tender touch seeped into the rest of his body.

Then fear, like a raging dragon rising from the depths of the earth, seemed to grab him. His heart was beating faster and faster until the pounding resonated in his ears.

'I don't want to be put into a home, that would be terrible, I'd hate it,' and Tom's voice shook with fear and his lower lip quivered.

'Listen Tom, there's no question of that. My friends and I

will sort you out. No one else will know, I promise. Don't worry. Before you know it you'll be all nice and cosy, and feeling much happier.'

'I can still come to Mokas, can't I?' and Tom looked at Bonnie appealingly.

Bonnie's voice was firm as she spoke to Tom, 'Of course you can, you're always welcome there, you know that. Now put those silly ideas out of your head and listen to me.'

Several months later the coffee shop door opened and Tom walked slowly over to his favourite seat by the window, his faithful stick tap-tapping on the floor beside him.

He looked quite dapper in his new trousers, shirt and pullover, his feet sitting comfortably in new brogues that made walking a lot easier. He hadn't realised wearing shoes two sizes smaller had been the cause of his hobbling. The chiropodist had worked wonders with his long-neglected feet and now he felt he had a spring in his step.

Tom's trip to the hairdressers had been quite an experience. He'd been surprised that the stylist hadn't turned her nose up at his greasy, tangled mass of hair. They'd even given him a nice cup of tea. He wasn't to know that Bonnie had explained things beforehand when she had booked the appointment.

People were very kind, he thought. Tears pricked the back of his eyes as he reflected over the last few months. So many people had helped to clear the flat, they'd all been so nice to him.

The day Bonnie had arranged for the flat to be fumigated he'd been taken to the cinema and then for tea. She'd never let on what was happening. Her friend Adam – who Tom could tell had a real shine for Bonnie – had let him stay at his flat for a week while the team of youngsters, and they were youngsters in his mind, cleared, cleaned, painted and re-arranged his flat until it looked bright, warm and welcoming. In fact, it felt as if it had been dragged out of the dark ages into modern times.

Bonnie's accompanying visit to his doctors had resulted in some fan-dangled medication that helped control his bladder during the night. Thankfully another benefit was that it lessened the times he regressed into the past. But he knew there was one more journey back in time to make. The thought of the memories filled him with dread, but he knew it was a necessary trip he had to embark on. He didn't know when it would happen, but he knew it would.

He jerked his mind back to the present. He'd never felt happier. Even Abigail had started to warm to him on his daily visits to the coffee shop.

One thing, however, that hadn't changed were the dripping cakes. They were still sadly dry and fruitless. He chuckled, turned to Bonnie and shouted, 'The usual please luv,' and he winked and smiled warmly at her.

'Right you are Tom, be with you in a jiffy.'

Abigail waltzed over to the counter, a smile spreading across her young face, picked up the tea and cake and walked over to Tom.

'There you are Tom, you enjoy your tea. The place wouldn't be the same without you, you know.' She walked quickly away to grab her make-up bag and plaster yet still more lipstick onto her already thickly coated lips.

The door opened again and an elegant grey-haired, elderly lady slowly walked over to the table he was sitting at. 'Hello,' she said kindly, and with a warm smile breaking across her face Maud sat down opposite Tom.

Bonnie had mentioned this kindly old lady to Tom one day. 'I was surprised when she told me where she lived Tom, right above you.'

A bold SOLD sign had stood for weeks for all to see outside the elegant Victorian house. Then one day he had watched a removal van; its contents of antique furniture were being carefully lifted out and taken into the depths of the first-floor flat. Several times he'd seen a smartly dressed elderly lady coming down the steps, always carrying a colourful bag in her gloved hand.

He'd avoided his neighbours at all cost. He often pressed himself against the basement wall, holding his breath so he'd be invisible. Sometimes he would walk around the square so that he wouldn't bump into this rather elegant-looking lady or the young professionals who occupied the other flats. Tom had felt so ashamed of his appearance. Yet he hadn't been able to jolt himself out of what the doctor had explained was depression resulting from the effects of his experiences on the front line. He'd had no energy or inclination to do anything about how he looked or the state of his home. But it was different now.

Tom had met Maud one day as he was just about to go down his steps; there was no avoiding her. It was like she had appeared out of nowhere. Bonnie hadn't had a hand in this either; it was purely down to fate really. Over the ensuing weeks they had become friends and Tom had even been to afternoon tea in Maud's spacious, light and airy flat. Her lemon drizzle cake had just melted in his mouth.

'Maud, how lovely to see you. I was just telling Bonnie how delicious your home-made cakes are,' and he grinned at her, his eyes dancing mischievously in their sockets.

'Oh go on with you Tom, you're just saying that so I'll make some more. Talking of cake ...' and Maud launched into her experiences as the finest cake maker in the local branch of the Women's Institute. 'Now Tom, when I ...' and Tom's eyes glazed over.

'I won't be here for a few days Tom,' Bonnie called out. 'But I'll be back Saturday. It's your big day, isn't it? Ninety eh? How amazing! Ninety!'

Suddenly the tunnel was again pulling him back. He tried to fight it but it was no good. It gripped him firmly and in the end he let go of all resistance and allowed the unfolding scene to became clearer in his mind.

He'd been whistling as he strolled through the familiar terraced streets on the suburbs of Islington, a multitude of memories stirring in his mind. Nothing had changed much, but then he hadn't really known what to expect. Returning from the front line wasn't something that happened often. He was so looking forward to seeing the little terrace with its chintz curtains. Although he hadn't heard from his wife Daisy or his son Edgar for a long time, he had just accepted that with a war on mail didn't always get through.

There was a rush of adrenaline, and his heart skipped a beat. He felt so excited as he turned the last corner. Not long now.

His whistling ended abruptly. He stopped dead in his tracks, his mouth gaping wide, and a shaky hand pushed back his hair. 'Christ, oh Christ. What the bloody hell?'

Standing like a statue he took in the scene of flattened houses. Both sides of the street and beyond were nothing but a pile of blackened rubble. Tears sprang out from his smarting eyes and he sank to his knees sobbing uncontrollably.

'Oh my God, oh my God. The whole lot's gone. Daisy, Edgar where are you?' His voice rang out and echoed eerily around, resounding off the piles of tumbled masonry.

He didn't hear the sound of heavy footsteps approaching. Tom was hardly aware of a weighty hand on his shoulder.

A voice started to penetrate through the dark. 'What's up mate? What's up?'

Tom looked up at the nondescript face of a man. 'It's all gone, all bloody gone. Where in God's name are my wife and son?'

'Sorry mate,' the stranger said in no uncertain terms as he helped Tom to his feet. He spoke in a matter-of-fact voice. 'Sorry, but it was a direct hit, see. They didn't stand a chance, the lot of them. There was nothing anyone could do. Not a thing. Sorry mate.' And the stranger swaggered off without a backward glance at the figure of a man destroyed by such unthinkable news.

Tom wandered around amongst the rubble for a while, shocked, dazed and distraught. He couldn't really remember what he did. He recollected waking cold and hungry, wondering where he was, and then the horror of what had happened to his Daisy and Edgar rushed back like an express train hitting him.

The stranger's voice echoed in his ears, 'A direct hit, didn't stand a chance!'

Somehow he'd got to a station and boarded a train. He'd come to when a ticket collector on the train shook him roughly.

'You'll have to get off here mate, end of the line.'

And that's what Tom did. Like a small, vulnerable child he alighted from the train, its thick smoke billowing along the draughty platform, the smell of the smoke etched deeply in his memory bank. Glancing around he'd looked at the large metal sign standing boldly alongside the platform. The name CHELTENHAM SPA stared back at him. Cheltenham, where the hell is that? he thought.

So began a new era of his life. He went through the long dark days like a robot, automated, numb, all that had happened securely placed in a locked box deep in the recesses of his mind, a chain and padlock firmly secured around his broken, bleeding heart, a shield in place as protection.

'So you see Tom,' and Maud's ramblings reached him through the fog. She hadn't even noticed the change that had come over him being so caught up in her recountings of Victoria sponges, fruitcakes and Bakewell tarts.

'Right then Tom, see you at three tomorrow, I'll have some nice butterfly cakes and gypsy creams ready for you. I've got a lot of baking to do for the pa …,' and with a startled look on her face she coughed and continued, 'oh, I mean the weekend.'

Having composed himself Tom was glad of the quiet and contemplated why Bonnie had asked to borrow a picture of his wife and son. She'd asked an awful lot of questions he realised now. At the time he hadn't noticed as Bonnie had a very chatty, easy-going personality. He realised that he'd related half his life history to her without even being aware of it.

He stood up, his faithful stick gripped securely in his now fattening hand, said his goodbyes and made his way slowly home. The iron railings decked in their new glossy coat and the freshly painted front door beamed a welcome at him. The key, now attached by a clip to his belt, slid easily into the lock and his spick and span home embraced him with warmth.

Bonnie and her friends had done an amazing job on the flat. His eyes smarted and he rubbed them with the back of his hand. Such kindness, such compassion had been shown to him by so many. He felt the warmth in his heart yet again and a glow filled him. But there was one part of his heart that he felt surely would never thaw. The faded sepia photograph of Daisy and Edgar looked back at him from the sideboard, and he remembered the precious days they had shared together. If only things had turned out differently. Ninety – who wants to be ninety? He remembered the numbers he'd crafted so carefully and stuck to the terrace's front door. Ninety was an easy number to make. The angular numbers had had pride of place on the door. Some of the neighbours had wanted Tom to make them for their homes, but he hadn't wanted to do that, they were special, just for his lovely family.

Easing himself down onto his new deeply cushioned sofa, Tom drifted into an uneasy sleep. Now and then groans escaped his parted lips as painful memories once more stirred deep within him.

Saturday dawned and there was a hive of activity in Mokas. Everything had been organised with precision. Bonnie had been amazed at the offers of help, not only in writing invitations, but also in making and contributing all kinds of delicious food and drinks. She wanted Tom's ninetieth birthday to be a wonderful occasion for him. She smiled to herself and patted the letter that had arrived from London that morning. A well of excitement filled her and she busied herself with rearranging yet again the array of scrumptious food that was spread across the tables.

Even the owner of the coffee shop had donated to Tom's festivities. Maud had been amazing and baked ceaselessly to produce cakes to die for.

In thirty minutes, Tom, oblivious to what was happening, would be arriving with Maud. She'd been clucking around him like an old hen the last few days, and it had really begun to irritate him. But she was a grand woman really, he just wasn't used to being fussed.

Tom's favourite table had a little lace cloth over it. Natasha, the part-time waitress, in one of her 'pelmet' skirts as old Tom referred to her mode of dress, had placed a jug of flowers on it, along with a little surprise wrapped carefully in bright paper.

Abigail, her make-up plastered even thicker than usual, although she didn't really need it, had also put a gift on the chair for him.

You could feel the buzz of excitement in the air as all the

guests were hiding in the far room. A screen had been placed in front of them to hide them from view. Bonnie had told them in no uncertain terms, to 'be as quiet as mice'.

The last to arrive had been the stranger from London. Good looking for sure, and although in his late sixties now he still could turn the heads of women.

Bonnie brushed a tear away and took a deep breath. She could see Maud with Tom walking alongside her, the faithful stick in his hand. They were turning the corner now. 'Right everyone, hush, he's coming.'

The excitement mounted and it hung in the air. It felt as though everyone was holding his or her breath.

With a clatter the door opened, and Maud, beaming in relief at having managed to keep the party a secret, led Tom dressed in his Sunday best over to his table. Before he reached it Bonnie had walked over and given him a great big hug. 'Happy birthday Tom, a very happy ninetieth birthday.'

It was a touching moment as they warmly embraced. 'Thank you Bonnie, thank you so much for all your kindness. I don't know where I would have ended up without your help.' He smiled and it was as if the smile appeared on his heart too.

Abigail and Natasha appeared. 'Hello Tom,' they chorused together. 'Happy birthday,' and they hugged him quickly. Tom was a little embarrassed at their openness.

'Well Tom,' Bonnie exclaimed, 'There are a few more people who want to make your day special. They all wanted to share it with you. I bet you didn't know you had so many friends.'

Natasha and Abigail drew the screen to one side.

Bonnie had a moment of panic. 'What if he has a heart attack?' and she turned to Maud for reassurance.

'Oh don't be so daft child, he's as strong as an ox. If he can cope with my constant chatter he can cope with this,' and they both laughed.

People began milling around. Once Tom had adjusted his eyes after taking in the sea of beaming faces, he began to focus and recognise people.

Why, there's Adam and all the youngsters from the youth group. They chorused 'happy birthday' to him, cheerful voices called out greetings and warm wishes. He hadn't noticed a strange-looking object covered by a sheet in the corner. Adam whipped the sheet off, and there was an old rocking chair. 'We thought you'd like this Tom. We knew you loved the old rocker you had years ago, so we hunted this one out for you. Everyone chipped in, and Bonnie didn't have anything to do with it either!' They all burst out laughing including Bonnie. She knew she was great at organising things and could be described as being a little bossy at times, but in a nice way.

He suddenly noticed Betty Parsons coming towards him.

'Hello Tom, happy birthday,' and she handed him a roughly wrapped parcel. Her frizzed, orange-coloured hair was no tidier than usual, but her warm smile embraced him. 'I've got an hour off from the launderette so I thought I'd just pop along and see you.'

'Thanks Betty.'

'Tom how did you manage to get to such a grand age?' Mr Love, the owner of Mokas asked. 'I'm sure I won't live that long. I didn't know what to get you, so I thought, that as you're my oldest customer, all your visits at weekends would be free. No, no buts,' and he waved his hand in the air refusing to take no for an answer.

Tom graciously accepted seeing the determined look on his face. 'Thanks, I really appreciate your generosity Mr Love.'

People were wandering around with plates of food now. Animated chatter and bubbly laughter filling the room.

Maud took Tom's arm and led him over to the well-stocked buffet. As Tom took in the array of delicious food spread on a crisp white tablecloth, his mouth began to salivate. There were dainty sandwiches: egg, cheese and pickle, ham and more, and each plate had a little flag stating what the filling was. Sausage rolls so small Tom could have put three in his mouth at once. Pineapple and cheese layered on cocktail sticks festooned out of a grapefruit. Vol-au-vents crammed with prawns, a smooth pink sauce spilling over the side of the pastry, looked invitingly at him. He read other labels: cheese straws, cheese and mushroom pizza, spinach and goats cheese tarts and so much more. 'A lot of fancy stuff,' he muttered under his breath. Nevertheless he licked his lips in anticipation of savouring the party fare.

Maud nudged his arm and showed him a delicious-looking birthday cake with an angular nine and a nought resting on the top. The cake took pride of place in the middle of the table. Around it there was an array of other tasty-looking small cakes, obviously fresh from Maud's kitchen.

'Tom, look, there are a lot more gifts for you over on that table and this is mine,' and she pressed a large, soft, gaily wrapped package into his hands. 'Happy birthday Tom,' and she kissed him tenderly on his cheek.

'Thanks Maud, thanks so much for all you've done.' A deep red flush began to spread up his neck and into his now filled-out cheeks.

Out of the corner of his eye he saw Bonnie walking towards him, a smartly dressed elderly stranger by her side.

Tom noticed his head of thick, curly brown hair and the deep-set hazel eyes. There was something about the way he moved. He had a slight limp, which meant he swaggered a little to one side.

Something stirred in Tom's memory of a young boy

running to meet him on one of his few trips home. Edgar had broken his leg and Daisy had written to him to explain that he would always have a slight limp. His heart seemed to somersault in his chest and a trembling began in his hands. He shuffled his feet and Maud reached out and steadied him.

The stranger was in front of him now. But was he a stranger? Tom's brain had difficulty in computing what was happening, it seemed to oscillate between 'he's a stranger', to 'but is he?'. Something familiar, something …?

Bonnie smiled into Tom's eyes, touched his arm gently and spoke softly. 'Tom, there's someone I want you to meet. Tom, this is Edgar.'

Father and son looked into each other's eyes knowing that the longing they had suffered and endured was melting away in that miraculous moment.

They embraced each other, and as Edgar spoke the words Tom had so longed to hear they echoed around in his head.

'Dad, oh dad …' Edgar's voice sounded cracked and there was moisture glistening at the corners of his eyes.

Tom's heart lit up. The padlock finally fell away, the shield disappeared, and the barriers had gone. A mixture of happiness and sadness enveloped them both as they stood holding each other.

Tom looked into his son's eyes, a reflection of his former self staring back at him, and with a cracked voice said, 'Welcome home son, welcome home.'

Dedication, determination, motivation and encouragement keep me going.

I came to realise when we read our literary masterpieces to each other that the feedback you receive is based on that person's perception, ideology and the style they scribe in. I nearly puked one night when someone suggested (no name mentioned of course) that I should change the word angels to aliens. No chance!

I felt very protective of my work, and although less reactive to criticism now can feel piqued at comments offered at times.

Self-belief is a staple diet for a writer. Mine has grown and something drives me forward to put this book together regardless of what others may think.

A Spiritual Experience

'So what are your plans for Christmas this year?'
'Oh, just the usual – I'm going up to see my mother in York.' She waited for him to extend the conversation, but nothing was forthcoming.

Oh well, disappointment again. She felt her stomach going into a knot and her hands began to tremble. She'd had such high hopes when she had met John. She remembered back to that night some months ago.

She'd walked into Happy Joe's café-bar and ordered her mocha. Picking the mug up from the counter she'd first slopped it over her hand and then in the confusion dropped her handbag, its contents spilling all over the floor.

The embarrassment of seeing those slinky red knickers sat among her deodorant and lipstick came flooding back. In a flash this man appeared as if out of nowhere. He bent down and picked the items up for her. As he held her red knickers on the end of his finger with them swinging like the pendulum of a clock, the whole place had erupted into laughter. 'Nice taste you have,' he said, smiling at her, and laughter crinkling at the corners of his mouth. She remembered thinking how kissable those lips looked. God it was so embarrassing to remember that incident and even now she could still feel the heat rising up her neck.

She heard someone clearing their throat and felt John's hand on her shoulder. A gentle touch that sent her heart racing. She had to shake her head to rid it of the fantasy she'd begun to drift into.

'Hey Sam, you seemed far away then, what were you thinking of? You had such a big smile on your face.' She blushed and turned to smile at him. His eyes really sparkled and as she looked at those, oh-so-kissable lips he leant over towards her, his hand outstretched and an intent look on his face. Oh, he's going to do it, he's going to kiss me at last. She quivered inside with the anticipation of their lips meeting. She felt a slight brush on her shoulder and realising she had her eyes closed opened them to see John bending forward concentrating on retrieving his drink from the bar.

As disappointment overwhelmed her she excused herself and marched off to the ladies. She'd never felt such anger before. Men usually came on really strong to her, but John was different: she never knew where she was with him, and it really irritated her. She delved into her handbag and drew out the red ribbons she had popped in earlier. As she tied her long, flowing tresses up high on her head and smoothed her new bright red lipstick over her sensuous lips, she winked at herself in the mirror. A quick spray of her new seductive perfume put the finishing touches to the new Sam. A girl has to pull out all the stops after all.

Feeling confident, relaxed and sexy she strolled back out into the bar. Several heads turned; even John did a double take as she climbed onto the bar stool and crossed her long legs. 'Sam,' her name sounded divine as it rolled off his tongue. 'Sam, I've been thinking.'

She gazed at him intently, 'Well,' she said, 'you've been thinking?'

'Well yes.' John seemed to stumble over his words. 'Oh to hell with it. Sam I don't know why I get so tongue-tied around you, it's never happened with any other girl I've dated before. I don't know what to do, say or how to behave when we're together. I spend hours imagining us having cosy meals in wonderful romantic restaurants. Then I visualise us walking along golden beaches under a tropical sky, or strolling hand in hand in the moonlight. But when we meet up I become this strange confused person I don't know. Sometimes I think someone's given me some sort of poison that has affected my thinking and the way I act. My brain's all fuddled. For Christ's sake Sam, what can I do?' He dropped his arms by his side in a hopeless gesture.

She slid slowly from the bar stool, taking the red ribbon from her hair and as her long, blonde locks cascaded down onto her shoulders she held the ribbon in both hands, threw it over his head and around his neck. Pulling him towards her she gently placed her lips on his and looked into his eyes.

The astonishment was clearly visible and as they moved apart he took her hands, sighed, looked longingly into her eyes, opened those sensuous lips, bent forward and whispered into her ear. 'This may sound crazy but I've fallen for you in a big way. Sam, I love you.'

She stood very still as tiny tears formed at the corners of her eyes and gently rolled down her cheeks. A smile spread across her face. 'Oh John, I love you too.'

He smiled, and reached into his pocket. 'Sam, I've been meaning to give you these back.' There dangling from his fingers were the slinky red knickers.

Her eyes nearly popped out of her head. Snatching them from him she stuffed them into her handbag and snapped, 'Boy you certainly take liberties, don't you!'

Her embarrassment was plain to see as she stalked from the bar throwing over her shoulder, 'Don't bother calling.'

He stood there, his mouth gaping open, his shoulders hunched with a look of astonishment on his face.

As the cold air hit her she said out loud, 'Well what was that all about?'

She'd felt so humiliated and fumed inside like a volcano waiting to erupt. Walking slowly home, with a heavy heart, her feet dragging along the damp pavement she turned the last corner and saw John standing under the lamp. How did he get here? He didn't even know where she lived.

'Sam, Sam, wait, I'm really sorry, truly I am. I didn't mean to embarrass you.'

'You mightn't have meant to embarrass me, but you blooming well did! I just wanted a great big hole to open and swallow me up. But how did you know where to come?'

'Well Sam, you may not believe this, but as soon as you had stormed off, I realised how stupid I had been. It being Christmas I started to think of angels and asked for help. It was really strange – as though I went into this invisible bubble and all the noise in the bar disappeared. A soft voice whispered to me "2 Constance Place" and then it felt like the bubble disappeared and the noise of the bar was around me again. So I just came. I guess you could describe it as a spiritual experience.'

They laughed, joined hands and walked up the path together, opened the front door and stepping inside stood before the beautifully decorated Christmas tree. 'Mmm, you know John, I think I had my own spiritual experience this morning. When I woke up there was this red ribbon lying on my pillow. I don't know how it got there, but somehow I knew to put it into my handbag.'

She held the red ribbon in her hand and placed it on the Christmas tree amongst the tinsel and lights.

'Happy Christmas Sam.'

'Happy Christmas John.' And their lips met once more.

Sometimes when the writing group gets together there isn't really a theme. It's a case of hoping inspiration will come. Free flowing, free forming. Freedom to get that next story down on paper. A lot of us struggled with this. However, if you let go of the fear something will usually emerge.

Hey, do you know? My grammar is crap. It's a constant trial for me to put dots, commas, semi-colons, asterisks and speech marks in the right place. And apostrophes, they're my worst nightmare. But then maths was my strong subject at school, not English. So I am reliant on friends to help me out and not beat myself up about it.

Never trust the spell check either – handing your power over to this box of electronic wisdom doesn't always pay off. It insists at times that a word should be spelt a certain way, but (gloat, gloat) when I check my faithful dictionary I find I was right all along.

Ripples

The tide was slowly receding and as the ripples of cold, brown water ebbed further away, sandbanks began to magically appear. This changing scene never ceased to amaze me and as I gazed in wonder the sound of the sea birds filled the air, their white wings sparkling as the sunlight caught them at every turn. The soft echo of wings moving in unison, taking that miracle called a bird round and round, soaring up high and then swooping to land graciously on the islands that were now being uncovered minute by minute.

I pulled my soft, warm hat down over my cold ears. A cosy knitted scarf was tied around my neck, and it brought a comforting warmth to my skin.

It had been a busy year and mum's death had moved me in ways I cannot describe. As I sang to her, her breath became more laboured and my heart beat faster. The fear mounted in my body, and my breathing became forced and difficult. The wind howled around the old house and branches from the old tree which grew close to the large sash window scratched backwards and forwards across the now rain-splattered glass.

But still I sang, my voice a little cracked, but still I sang. My hands a little shaky, but still I sang. My heart thudding nosily in my chest, but still I sang.

I looked at the tired old bony form of this person who had given me life. Who'd shown me little love, who'd never really wanted me. But wanted everything from me. Whose jealousy had been so evident when her bright witch-like eyes had flashed at me with scorn on occasions.

But still I sang as tears fell in a ceaseless motion as I opened my heart in an act of forgiveness and thanked her for giving me life.

Suddenly the temperature in the room dropped and I shivered then pulled the blanket tighter around my tense body as I sensed a presence there with us. The Angel of Death had arrived. It was so!

Her breath was now struggling to find a way into the skeletal form that lay beneath the starched white sheets. There were long gaps between each rasping breath. As the silence went on I thought, 'This must be the last breath for ever for this person.' But then a shudder and air was dragged once more down into her throat and into well-worn lungs.

I stopped singing and one huge rasping breath drew in, struggled out and all was still and quiet. The empty form lay before me, the shell of a once alive person resting now. Never would it take another breath, never would another word be uttered from those lips, never would a step be taken by those feet, never would those cold, glacial eyes look at me with disdain.

It was complete, the tide had turned.

I calmed, my breathing eased, my body relaxed and I prayed for the safe journey of this soul into the light. The temperature rose in the room and all was calm, all was still.

A tiny warm hand wriggled its way into mine. The young, excited voice echoed out across the now distant water.

'Na Na. Na Na, come on we're ready now.' Chloe's big eyes looked up at me and I pushed the memories of a bygone life away.

'Come on darling, let's get warm around the camp fire.' Her brother Andrew came and took my other hand and we went and crouched around the flickering flames, our skewers securely holding the fluffy pink and white marshmallows as they sizzled in the heat.

We are but the ripples of life. Changing, growing, flowing.There is constant movement, and the cycle of death and rebirth is continuous. Here in this moment I am a ripple of my mother; my children a ripple of me and I look with loving eyes on my grandchildren who are the a ripples of my children. A continuation through time. And so the generations flow on.

With joy and love in my heart I turned to these two precious children and spoke. 'Come on, let's sing,' and three clear happy voices sang, our voices ripples of sound floating out across the void to be caught by the wind and taken up to soar with the birds.

Here we go again, the dreaded curve balls. Nasty little words that have to be woven into our stories. There is always a degree of anticipation, some consternation and, having become anally retentive lately, 'constipation'.

The challenges of a writer are numerous, but never lose faith. Keep going!

By the way some of these stories were finished the same evening and were whisked away to be edited, and re-edited. Not just by me, but by friends too.

The worst challenge was to complete the ending of my first ever story to emerge. The working title we were given – Indecision – well, that theme followed me along the way and it wasn't until six months down the line that an ending appeared. So, beware of titles.

Look what happened as I was writing this! Out of blue came yet another monologue.

Curve balls a-coming
Short and sweet
Nasty little things I don't greet

What will they be?
Appropriate or not
There ain't no choice about it
Hope they won't be grot

Ah ha, it's just perfect
It fits just right
Curve balls I love you
In fact you're a delight

Knocking on Heaven's Door

How tired she felt, as she walked that last hundred yards home from the bus stop. Her feet throbbed and her back ached as she climbed the stone steps to her front door. In fact, she realised she was exhausted. It was always good to see that door, a familiar sight that spelled security, a place to escape the world. Behind the door lay a haven of tranquillity where she could be herself and take off the mask she wore in her everyday life. It was something she had got used to wearing now for protection, her way of dealing with the way things were right now.

The key turned easily in the lock and once through the door a sense of relief come over her. As she turned and pushed it shut, the sound of the constant traffic faded into the background.

'Ah, peace and quiet. Just what I need,' she mumbled.

Flicking the switch, a shower of light filled the hallway and then instantly disappeared. The exasperation was clear in her voice as she exclaimed out loud, 'Damn, the *light bulb*. That's the third in two days to have blown. Why do things always seem to happen in threes?'

Susan kicked off her shoes that had become tight on her aching, hot feet. She went into the kitchen and turned on the kettle.

'You'd think, working in a shoe shop, I'd be able to find a pair of shoes that stayed comfortable all day.'

Her feet had become more swollen in the last few weeks, and at times she'd wondered whether she should give up her job.

The sound of the kettle was a comfort to her. She made her usual pot of Earl Grey and laid it out, with an intricately decorated tray cloth, on a carved wooden tray. This ritual really helped her to unwind. It denoted the end of a long, arduous day. How customers could be so amazingly tiresome was beyond her.

The egocentric retired colonel Barnaby Rudge (Old Fudge as he'd been nicknamed) had been in today. Anyone would think he'd eaten a pound of plums by the way he spoke. It was obvious to all that he hadn't realised he'd left the army years ago. Susan was sure one day he would prod her with that cane he carried. He had this tiresome way of jabbing it at whomever he was speaking to. The 'staff' was a keepsake from his days as a staff sergeant in the army. Everyone ended up dancing from side to side to avoid being the recipient of the jab. He gave the impression that he still thought himself on the parade ground. He had this horrible way of barking at people as if they were minions, and expecting them to jump to attention.

Her colleague, Millie, often complained that he never put on clean socks and when he pulled off his shoes Millie's nose would wrinkle and her hand would dive in her pocket for the scented handkerchief which she kept at the ready. Susan had learned this trick pretty quickly from Millie when she first worked in the shoe shop. Must have hanky at the ready!

'Now I'm sounding like the colonel,' she thought.

She knew now not to exchange looks with Polly the young shop assistant when Old Fudge came into the shop. Once they had sniggered and the colonel had flushed red up his neck, his eyes nearly popping out from their sockets. His moustache had danced around on his face as a sneer appeared on his blood-red lips, which only resulted in making their sniggers grow even louder.

Miss Dauncey, the shop manager, had not been very impressed with their behaviour and they had had a right telling off. But there was a twinkle in her eye when she told them they should be more polite and tolerant of their customers' quirky ways.

Today there were no problems with smelly socks, but the stench of alcohol had gushed out on his breath. Lunch at the club with his cronies, a bottle or two of red wine and all was lost. His slurred voice and blood-shot eyes resulting from the whisky chasers made her shiver. Boy, did he give her the creeps.

Snuggling into the cushions on the sofa, she felt the warmth from the soft fabric. It was a real comfort for her tired body. The sofa was the one luxury in her lounge on which she had had no hesitation in spending some of her inheritance. Gradually she could feel her mask slipping away, becoming more herself. It's hard to be polite when customers are so irritating.

'Yes sir, certainly, I'll have a look for you madam, no problem miss.'

'Ahhhhhhh!' she screamed. 'I hate it, I hate it!'

Oh to be in a job where she had fun, excitement and yes, lots of money. If it wasn't for her mother's inheritance she would still be living in that gloomy bed-sit down on Lysons Avenue. With a deep shudder and a cold chill running up her spine she sighed.

'What's the point of dreaming any more?'

Then there was dear old Matilda Mouse (Mrs Simmons really). A real regular Nora Batty, stockings and home-made elastic garters. The first time Matilda Mouse had come into the shop and her stockings had tumbled in creases to her ankles, Susan had had to dash to the loo before her laughter burst out and tears rolled down her face.

Oh my goodness, what about 'orrible 'enry? The most obnoxious child she'd ever met. His mother totally doted on 'enry and would sing his praises as he caused havoc in the shop. Susan had never seen or met such an indulged child. Boxes hit over, shoes turned out as he rushed around screaming, 'No! Don't want those shoes! I want the others.'

He'd stamped his foot in defiance one day and even his mother lost her cool and hit him round the head with her *newspaper*.

'What I'd like to do to 'enry is nobody's business,' Susan thought.

She started to laugh. She laughed so much she cried until her sides ached.

'Well, I suppose my job's not boring is it?'

She went over to the mantelpiece and picked up the picture frame that held her mother's photo. So young to die, sixty years old and having a real zest for life. And then she was gone. She still missed her so much, even after two years. At times she was sure she felt her mother with her, but usually dismissed it as her imagination playing tricks with her.

'Thanks, mum, for everything you did for me. You always loved to hear about the customers that came into Graingers. We'd laugh together and enjoy the fun of devising nicknames for them all.'

She smiled as she wandered to the window. A sad feeling welling up in her, her eyes began to smart. She'd felt quite hot and a little shivery at work and hoped she wasn't getting a cold. She remembered they'd told her to avoid getting colds at all costs and went quickly to get some of the *remedy* that was kept in the bathroom cabinet.

As she walked back through the hallway that strange giddy feeling came over her again. It was happening much more frequently now. Shaking her head, hoping the feeling would pass, she became aware of the sound of music floating everywhere, softly at first and then a little louder. It was a lilting melodious sound that seemed to swirl and swirl around her. The hallway began to fill with light and a warm glow came over her. She felt peaceful, happy and light, almost as if she was floating. Gradually she became aware of a faint figure. Able to recognise the face of her mother, she stepped forward with her hands outstretched.

'That's strange, I feel so light, as though I don't weigh anything.'

The light became brighter and brighter and the form of her mother became so much clearer. Her smiling face seemed to call Susan and she stepped forward with ease and together they floated up and out through the roof of the house.

It was like someone was pulling her upward on an invisible silver cord. There was no escaping the pull. It was the most amazing feeling, impossible to describe, as she drifted up and up. Angels appeared around her, dressed in robes and with a multitude of coloured lights shining intensely from them, their huge feathered wings stretched out as if to protect her. The light was so soft, so gentle as it enveloped her. She felt so safe. It was as though she was knocking on heaven's door. As the silver cord suddenly loosened and fell quickly away, snaking through the light and disappearing from sight, an immense sense of freedom came over her.

Before her eyes a huge ball of golden light appeared, and hovered near her, gradually growing in intensity. The light shimmered, sparkled and shone and gradually enfolded her. She became a part of it, she was it, and there was no separation from it. All she felt was immense love, incredible love, filling her, taking her over and then bliss, pure bliss. Then came a feeling of being home. At last she had found what she had been searching for all her life. Her mother, her father, gran and granddad Powell and many more of her family were gathered there to welcome her. They seemed to shimmer and glow, change shape, but still she knew who they were.

There had been, on occasions before, momentary feelings like this. One day she had smelt the roses, damp with dew, in Friars Gardens, a local memorial garden she liked to wander in when things got her down. A moment of bliss, wonder and then it was gone. This time she knew it was not going to go, this was going to last forever and ever.

Some days passed before the police were called when she hadn't turned up for work. They had to break down the door to get in, and as the door crashed open they had found her lying in a crumpled heap on the hall floor. It was said that it was still possible to make out the look of amazement on her face and the smile that radiated from her lips. Rumours were rife at work of course as to how she died. Some blamed drink, others said that she had died of a broken heart. But her diary told it all.

March 6th: It's hard to believe I may only have a few months to live. I've got to go on, find a mask that helps me through each day until it's time. I am sure mum and I will meet again and hopefully then I will be at peace. In fact I know that it will be the most incredible experience of my life!

Liggy's voice, cheerful as usual, said, 'This evening, everyone …'

With bated breath I waited. It was still early days for the writing group, but in fact these early months had passed quickly. And still I could write. Now, though, it was more serious, we'd got braver with our feedback. Well, in fact some had become very direct and skin hadn't thickened as it needed to. You do need to believe in yourself, take on board what feels right, cast aside comments that don't fit and just go on.

'… we are going to write about superstition.'

How unlucky can that be? How do you write about superstition?

Well, we were given a slip of paper, or rather we chose our slips. And what do I get? 'If you drop a card it's unlucky.'

With a positive frame of mind I set to work and I just love how this story evolved.

Superstition – A Load of Old Codswallop

My grandfather, an old cynic, referred to my grandmother's obsession with superstitions as a bunch of old wives' tales.

There he was again, muttering under his breath. You couldn't make out what he was saying but you could darn well guess.

He was always the same where my grandmother was concerned, and it had gradually got worse over the years. His jowls now hung loose and his yellowed false teeth jumped around in his snarling mouth. It wasn't a pretty sight to witness when he went off on one of his turns.

He could never take my grandmother seriously, but time and time again her superstitious nature had proven invaluable in either avoiding bad luck or being able to bring fortune on the family.

And what a family it was. Grandfather was a North Country person through and through; strong, tough and definitely set in his ways. You could never get him to see another's point of view, while my grandmother, although a northerner herself, had a gentler, softer nature and a grand sense of humour, and she needed it too, living with grandfather. In later years though, she had become bitter. Who could blame her. He had led her a right merry dance for sure.

They were two embittered oldies living together, or perhaps existing together was more like it, in that hovel in Lugs Lane down by the Brakenside canal. It was damp, old and tumbling down around their ears, but life seemed to somehow carry on.

The smell from the canal on a hot summer's day was something you just wanted to escape. My nostrils used to flap in and out at an incredible rate as if trying to blot the smell out, but somehow it seeped in and filled my chest and then hit my stomach like a sack of manure fresh from the dung heap. I would heave and want to throw up, so I had devised a way of gulping in some fresh air further back and running as fast as I could with my skirts held up above my knees. I wouldn't take a single breath and I'd reach my grandmother's gasping for air and she would laugh her socks off and exclaim, 'Oh Em, you look right funny, you do!'

My grandmother had always described me as a bit of a rascal, full of life and cheeky with it. I had long, wavy brown hair that fell in tangles down my back and when I ran it streaked out behind me like a flowing mane.

I remember the day she came hobbling into the house, her craggy face creased in a scowl that seemed to stretch from ear to ear. Cackling she was, like an old haggard witch about to try her latest potion on some poor unsuspecting person.

'That's it,' she croaked, 'I knew it, just knew it. That black cat has gone and got itself killed. I can't believe it, I can't. Now there's a sign of bad luck for sure. I always knew I'd have good luck when that cat crossed my path.'

'Shut up you blathering old woman, you. You're an addled old hag, addled I say. No such thing as bad luck,' and my grandfather stomped out through the back door to the privy in the backyard. As he pulled the rotten, old wooden door open, it flew off its rusty hinges, creaking and groaning. It knocked him flat, it did! With his arms flailing in the air, he landed on his back in the mud.

Grandmother and I stood in the doorway laughing until our sides ached and tears streamed down our faces.

'No such thing as bad luck then?' we cried and went inside to sup our mugs of thick, steaming tea. I tried hard to control my laughter, but it was no good. I remember spluttering my tea all over her table.

'Do you remember that day up the Pig and Whistle Em?' Grandmother chirped. 'You know, that day your grandfather knew he was on to a winner in the card game? He insisted he was going to go, even though my tea leaves spelled trouble.'

As she continued, her voice became more and more excited. 'Would he listen? No! That cantankerous old bugger thinks he knows everything. Well, I warned him I did, loud and clear my warnings were, but alas they fell on deaf ears. Bah. Of course, being his obstinate old self he didn't take a bit of notice of your grandmother, did he? I said to him, I did, "Mind when you play you don't drop one of them cards; a real bad omen it is. Brings bad luck for sure."

'"Shut your mouth woman, you're mad," he growled back. What did he go and do? Spent an hour before the game supping that silly old landlord's home-made cider and, hardly able to stand, set himself to play. Well he couldn't control the drool from that big old mouth of his. And those great big, gnarled fingers always made him clumsy. Them fingers that hadn't attempted an honest day's work for nigh on seventy years you know! He dropped two of them bloody cards, not one, but two!' Grandmother started laughing and held her sides as she spluttered the rest of the story out. 'Old Billy Finch picked up the two cards and with deft fingers swapped them for two of his own he did. Bloody cheek, I say.

'Well he lost good and proper too, and all them lot in the pub had a good old laugh at his expense for sure. Not only that, he lost the week's housekeeping money too. I had to beg from my friends, I did. Hung my head in shame having to do that you know, love, hung my head in shame.'

Her voice was now nothing more than a squeak and I had to listen carefully to catch her words.

'And then what happened when he got up at the end of the game? Well, I would have enjoyed being there to see it. This is how the story goes, though it has changed a bit down the years, mind you.

'As he staggered from his chair, the leg dropped off. He stumbled over, hit his chin on old Daffy's knee and his false teeth shot out across the floor. They were never the same after that they weren't. You should have seen the look on old Cracker's face. He was the landlord's shaggy old dog. He snarled for sure and then ran off and hid behind the bar, right scared he was. Old Fred Toomey had to half carry your grandfather home, he did. Someone had shoved his false teeth into one of his pockets and all, right covered in fluff and hairs they were too. Took a good old soak in the bicarbonate to get them clean again.'

Just then there was a banging and a coughing in the doorway and we were brought back to my grandfather stumbling in through the back door, covered in mud and drooling spittle from the side of his puckered mouth. There was a large damp patch on his trousers where he'd peed himself. I had to pinch myself to stop from going into hysterics, I did.

'Fancy a game of cards, Grandfather? You might have a bit of luck this time!'

Grandmother and I looked at each other, collapsed into each other's arms laughing and crying while Grandfather muttered loudly, 'Superstition, a load of old codswallop it be.'

'Never learn, will he Em?'

I choked out my reply. 'No I don't think he will.'

We picked up our mugs and went on supping our tea, while grandfather, a-cursing and a-swearing, stomped off up the old staircase leaving a trail of muddy footprints in his wake.

A Grave Experience

The spade, freshly sharpened, cut its way into the dark, damp soil. It had a certain smell to it that always made Davey's nose wrinkle. It wasn't unpleasant but somehow it started his nose dripping and he had to use the sleeve of his old, stretched, baggy, woollen jumper to wipe the droplets away.

Being a gravedigger wasn't a normal sort of a job. In fact, you could describe it as being ceaselessly boring. Spade after spade of claggy soil being thrown up and out. The constant, repetitive movement brought a dull ache to his shoulders and he'd often stop, lean on his spade and shrug his shoulders up and down to ease the pain. Yet for big old Davey there was a sense of satisfaction in seeing this last resting place take shape for someone's poor departed relative.

It didn't scare Davey when he finally dug down to the last layer and found himself standing on soggy ground. He didn't always think things through and had ended up in a few situations that gave the local gossips something to talk about. Once it had rained so much it had been really difficult to scramble out.

Old farmer George had passed by that day. It was his old sheepdog Nes who had raced over barking and whining.

Davey wondered if old Nes had thought he was one of the sheep who had escaped from High Fell. Farmer George had a right laugh at Davey's predicament. He had rushed to get reinforcements from the Old Bull Inn, which stood next to the churchyard.

The grave today, however, was different, and there were tears spilling from Davey's eyes as he climbed up the old wooden ladder which this time he had fortunately remembered to bring with him.

He'd just dug the last resting-place for his Granny Proctor. Being ninety-three was an achievement and he couldn't really have expected her to live much longer, but Davey had never experienced losing someone he'd loved. In fact he was an orphan and had been left on the church steps one cold winter night. If it hadn't been for the fact that the Reverend Peter Miles had gone back to lock up the church he could have frozen to death. Folks in the village often referred to him as the 'foundling'.

It was strange though, Davey never felt the cold and could wander the moors in the depths of winter with no hat and coat and never suffer any ill effects.

He remembered Christmas Eve a few years back. There had been a howling east wind blowing over the moors. Farmer George had supped far too many double whiskies that evening and had only managed to stagger as far as the snug door before his legs had given out on him. So it was good old Davey who had charged off into the dead of night when the sheep needed to be brought down from High Fell. Neither the wind howling in his ears nor the driving snow catching in his hair seemed to bother him. He was gone for well over three hours, but he didn't suffer any ill affects at all and there was a big cheesy grin on his rosy-cheeked face when he had eventually got back to the inn.

Percy, the miserable, moaning, grumpy landlord was

heard to say to some of his old cronies, 'Charmed, that's what he is, charmed.'

Quite a few of them had nodded in agreement. Well they would, wouldn't they, being chums of old Percy.

It had been decided when Davey was found that being cared for by Granny Proctor, a homely, kind sort of a woman, was the best thing for him. Mind you, she did have a reputation in the area for being a bit of a witch. When really all it was, was that she was able to use the hedgerow plants to mix medicinal, as she called them, concoctions for all sorts of ailments.

'Only old folklore,' she used to chuckle.

Old Billy Smith, the smithy, had had a large carbuncle on his backside once, and Granny Proctor had made a burning hot poultice using one of her tried and tested potions. It stank to high heaven and when young Tom, the blacksmith's apprentice, had been told to slap in on Billy's backside, his screams could be heard in the village square. Tom had enjoyed inflicting this pain on his master, who at times was real mean to him. He had even been known to thrash Tom with his old leather belt.

Billy wasn't very welcome in the Old Bull for the next week as a terrible stench emitted from his old, baggy trousers. He was well known for not being overly keen about washing himself, anyway. Folks weren't quite sure though, whether it was the poultice or the pickled onions that the old blacksmith had a liking for that caused the smell. Billy was a bit thick and never did work out why people avoided him; even his dog Flame had kept out of his way and had hid in the corner of the bar.

Davey stood and gazed into the deep, dark hole. Raindrops were starting to fall steadily now. He began to feel concerned and scratched his head as he listened to the plip, plop of the rain as it began to settle in the bottom of the freshly dug grave. He couldn't bear to think of his Granny's coffin sitting in a pool of water. 'I'll have to bail it out in the morning if it's still there,' he muttered. 'I don't want her getting a chill.'

He turned, and walked slowly along the gravel path, a forlorn look on his face. Making his way back to the cottage he had shared with her for the last thirty plus years wasn't a happy thing to do any longer. His hair was soaking now and droplets of water fell down his neck and onto his eyelashes, forcing him to blink.

As he pushed open the old, creaking, wooden gate, with the name Briar Cottage hanging crookedly on it, his heart felt heavy. No lights streamed out from the cottage windows and there wasn't any smoke billowing out of the crooked chimney pot.

Although the reverend's wife had brought Davey over some food, it wasn't the same as his Granny's cooking. She'd been real nifty in the kitchen had Granny. But then life had its twists and turns and this was one of those turns that hurt and left you wondering what the hell would happen next.

He let himself in, the old key turning easily in the lock of the cottage door, the smell of the rambling roses that cascaded down around the door permeating the damp air. As he stepped into the dark, cold parlour, a dejected feeling was hanging heavy in his heart.

'Ah, there you are Davey,' a familiar voice said. 'I was beginning to worry about you. I must have dozed off, and when I woke up it was dark.'

His grandpa stood up, stretched himself, walked over to Davey and put his arm round his shoulders.

'Come on Davey, I know it's hard but we've got to adjust to not having Granny around. Once the funeral is over I am sure it will get better. It's not easy is it? Seeing her here in the parlour lying in a coffin. A right character she was for sure, wasn't she? She would have wagged her tongue at me for sure for not having the fire burning and the kettle steaming on the hearth.

'Well now Davey, wash them there hands, they're as black as soot. Come on now. Then go and look in the corner of the parlour, be quick, there's a good lad.'

Hands washed, Davey rushed to the corner of the room nearly colliding with Granny's coffin on the way. His eagerness to find out what he was supposed to look at had made him clumsy. There to his surprise, curled up on a bit of old blanket, was a tiny sleeping puppy.

Grandpa spoke firmly. 'She needs careful looking after now, so make sure you take care of her or your granny will be banging her stick on the floor like she used to when she was annoyed.'

'All right, Grandpa,' said Davey, and he picked up the puppy, cuddling it close to his body, a smile on his face.

Somewhere in his mind a memory stirred of a tiny, helpless baby lying on a cold church step under a starry sky. He hugged the puppy close, stroking its soft curly fur and said, 'You're safe now, you're safe now little puppy. Grandpa can I give it a name? Oh please,' Davey exclaimed.

'Well Davey, what do you think you would like to call her? It's a girl mind you.'

'Gem, Grandpa, Gem,' Davey said breathlessly. 'You see it's Granny's name backwards. Meg turned around see, GEM!'

'Well, well you never cease to amaze me Davey, who would have thought you could work that out. That's a grand name lad, Gem it will be.'

Fred looked over at the still form of his beloved Meg. He was sure he could see a smile on her face and he was convinced he heard her voice whisper in his ear.

'You did the right thing Fred, definitely the right thing.'

'Thank God for that, woman, you were always telling me

off when you were alive. I never did anything right, and now you've gone you're singing me praises.' He scratched his head, laughed and said out loud, 'Never understand women, I won't.' And he walked over to Davey with a big smile on his face.

It's a Miracle, isn't it?

'Joy of the beholden
fear of the abyss
taken to my heart in light
sworn by angels winged flight
now the transformation takes place
in light of heaven, be my named sake
in God-like image going forth to tell
the world and all of divine power
of seeking deep inside our truth
where search has ended full and timely
as soul-like we walk the passive earth in joy and peace .'

'Oh for Christ's sake Peter, will you stop this bloody crap.'

'Sorry Daphne but you know I love to let my thoughts just flow, and saying it out loud seems to take me to places where I can escape.'

'Don't be so childish Peter, and yes, I know you like your escapism, but it's not going to help in this situation, is it? We've just got to face it, something has to be done about Grandfather.'

'Obviously Daphne, but it's not easy is it? It's a real sad state of affairs.'

Peter, with a haggard look on his face began muttering, 'I remember how Grandfather used to play with us when we were little. Swinging us round, throwing us in the air and catching us. I can feel now how wonderful it was. I used to squeal with delight. It's so clear still, almost as if I am back there experiencing it all over again. That feeling of excitement, as I fell through the air, his strong, powerful hands catching me and placing me gently on the ground.'

Peter's eyes misted over. 'It's so hard to think that such a fine, strong, energetic man has ended up old, bent, confused and not able to look after himself. He's even started dribbling now, and his eyes seem to have a glazed, vacant look at times. The other day he couldn't remember what my name was.' Peter's voice was hardly audible and he looked at Daphne in desperation.

Daphne sighed, shook her head and found there was a big hard lump in her throat. She had to force her words out, and at first they struggled to get from her mouth and form into any sensible meaning. 'What I'm trying to say,' she began again, after yet another attempt at clearing her throat. 'Is, is …' she paused, feeling a tear start to glide gently down her cheek. It felt hot and seemed to burn slightly as it made its slow journey across her skin. As she brushed it away, she was aware her mascara had left streaks of black over her face. She noticed Peter's eyebrows rising in a quizzical gesture.

'What the hell are you looking at me like that for?'

'Sorry Daphne,' Peter exclaimed, 'but you've smudged your mascara and it's all over your face.' He was wearing that stupid schoolboy grin and she could feel the heat rising up the back of her neck.

Daphne mentally clocked that she should have bought the

waterproof mascara recommended to her by the assistant on the make-up counter in Frosters department store. But she'd been such a stuck-up bitch that Daphne hadn't wanted to give her the pleasure of an expensive sale, so she had ended up buying some cheap crap.

She eased herself up from the armchair and walked over to the mantelpiece and picked up Grandfather Harper's photograph. He did look fine in his army uniform, a real stalwart of a man, so straight and tall with dark brown hair. She could even see the twinkle in his eyes, although he was trying to look really serious.

'It was wonderful when Grandfather took me out that day, do you remember? I think it was the spring of eighty-nine. Of course, you were away then weren't you, travelling Australia with Andrew Fraser. It's strange how clear it all seems to me.

'Well, he took me to pick bluebells in old farmer Scott's woods. I don't think I will ever forget the happiness I experienced that day. We'd ambled across the fields and snuck through that old rotting gate at Castle End Lane. Then Grandfather told me to close my eyes. I didn't dare peep as he watched me so closely. I could tell we had left the field by the crunch of twigs under my feet. The air seemed cooler too, and although my eyes were tightly shut I sensed it had become darker.

'Grandfather suddenly said, "Come on now my little princess, open your eyes."

'I can't explain how it felt when I opened my eyes. I had to rub them to get them to focus properly. The floor of the wood was carpeted in bluebells. The sun was filtering down through the trees and the leaves caused mosaic patterns to dance over the woodland floor as a breeze, so gentle, shook the trees and stirred their new spring growth. I flung myself into Grandfather's arms laughing and giggling, "Oh

Grandfather it is magical, do you think there are fairies and pixies here?"

'He looked at me with those wonderful hazel eyes of his and said, "I am sure there are princess, let's sit down and see if we can see them. We have to be very, very still."

'So we sat still for what seemed like hours until Grandfather broke the silence, squeezed my hand, stroked my hair and turned to me saying, "You'll never forget this moment princess, seeing the wonder of nature in all her fine glory, it will stay with you forever."

'I am sure he had tears in his eyes too. He helped me pick bunches and bunches of bluebells and we took some to the churchyard to put on Gran's grave and the rest we took home to Mum. I told her that we'd seen the fairies and pixies dancing in the wood. She smiled as I went on to say that the birds had flown down and sung so beautifully for them to dance to. There were tiny wrens, and brilliant blue-black blackbirds, mistle thrushes with their speckled chests and robins whose scarlet coats shone bright. The little people had twirled and whirled around, and if you listened very carefully you could hear their laughter. Their tiny fairy wings reflected the sunlight in all directions.

'Grandfather smiled at me, winked and said, "It was a magical fairy glade."

'The pixies' small, coloured hats had bobbed and bounced and although they kept tugging them back onto their heads some had managed to fall off. Mr Magpie had picked them up in his beak and placed them into a pile for the pixies to collect later.

'Mum gathered me up in her arms and exclaimed, "Oh I wish I had been there to see them too darling."

Peter stood up, walked over to Daphne, and putting his hand gently on her shoulder said. 'Who's lost in fantasy now then? Come on, we've got to collect Mum and take her to see the nursing homes we've decided to look at.'

Daphne, at twenty-three years of age usually bright, alive and vibrant, sighed, 'I've never thought of Grandfather getting old, and it's made me realise I'm older too.'

Grandfather had been such a source of support when she'd struggled at school. Being bullied was no joke and the teachers didn't pay any attention to the complaints she had made about nasty Shirley Clements and her toady friends. But Grandfather had gone up there after school one day, when all the kids had left, and told old bungling Mr Parish the headmaster that something had to be done. Not next week, next month, or in six months' time, but this week, in fact tomorrow! Grandfather had no time for old Parish. He'd told Daphne his handshake was like a wet piece of halibut off a fish-monger's slab. In less than a week the bullying had stopped, and although that Clements girl still gave her sly looks on occasions she'd left her alone.

Peter interjected, 'Yeah, he used to have a way of sorting things out and bringing a little humour into the most difficult of situations. He made me laugh so much Daphne when he told me about the day Gran died.'

Peter, with a wistful look in his eyes, went on to relate the story. 'When the undertakers were lifting her into the coffin somehow her false teeth shot out and there was a mad scramble to find them. They'd slipped right under that enormous chest of drawers. You know, the one that stood under the window. Poor Gran had to be put back on the bed while they all heaved and pulled at the chest to get at them.

'She was a sly one our gran, wasn't she?' Peter exclaimed. 'Grandfather would never have known she'd hidden that old biscuit tin under there stuffed with fivers and coins. Grandfather told me he'd exclaimed in a fit of mirth, "Well that's where the old so and so had hidden my beer money."

'Apparently he turned to his Ethel and exclaimed, "Can't

stop me now can you Eth? I'm going to have some right good evenings with my old mates down the British Legion."

'Her teeth forgotten, they packed her off in the coffin and as the hearse was driving away Grandfather came rushing out the door, holding her teeth aloft, shouting, "Wait wait." Apparently the faces of the undertakers were a sight to behold.

'Oh well, we'd better be off, we're late already. You've got the list haven't you Daffers?'

'Don't call me that, you know I hate it,' Daphne shouted with an indignant look on her face.

'Sorry, Daffers, um, I mean Daphne, let's get going.'

Their mum was standing at the kitchen sink when they arrived at Branksby Cottage. Cotton, their old black and white cat, was curled up in her basket near the Aga. She raised her head slightly, peered from sleepy green eyes and then closing them again settled down to sleep the sleep of sleep, that only cats seem able to do.

Daphne and Peter affectionately hugged their mum in turn. They knew she'd been crying again; her eyes were red and puffy. 'I can't do this, I just can't,' she exclaimed. 'Your grandfather has lived here with me for twenty years now since your father was killed. How can I put him in a home, he'll hate it. I'm already feeling guilty just thinking about it.'

'Come on Mum,' they both chorused. 'We've got no choice. You know what the consultant told us, he's going to deteriorate and will need twenty-four-hour nursing care.'

She burst into tears. 'I don't know what I'm going to do without him. He's been so supportive over the years and so good to you two. He always seemed to know the right thing to say. He certainly calmed me down a time or two when I got into a right pickle over some of your escapades.'

'We weren't that bad, Mum,' Daphne shouted, throwing her head back in a haughty gesture as she spoke.

Peter looked sulky and muttered something under his breath.

'Sorry both, it's not the time to recollect your younger day rebellions, is it? No, there isn't a choice, is there? We don't have the money to fund round-the-clock nursing care, so a social services' placement in a home it's got to be. We'd better be off.'

Three forlorn-looking people dragged themselves out of the kitchen and got into the car. They all felt sad but knew they had to find out what these homes were like. Maybe there would be one that was suitable and would provide the best possible care for Grandfather.

They had decided on three homes, each within a fifteen-mile radius of the cottage, and fortunately they were all in rural locations. One in particular looked really pleasant and had lots of grounds where the residents could be taken under supervision. The head of home had sounded really nice when Daphne had telephoned her, and she could tell from her manner that she had been really sympathetic about their dilemma.

'Don't worry,' Mrs Phillips had said. 'It's quite normal to be feeling this way. Come along and have a look, you don't need to have an appointment. I am here most days but my deputy Mrs Collins can always talk to you and show you round if I'm not available.'

The Pines did have a nice ring to it, Daphne thought.

All too soon they had arrived at The Pines, so named because of a row of impressive pine trees that towered behind the old Victorian house. The picture on the brochure had looked nice, but now they were there the trees seemed to give a mysterious look to the building.

She became aware of Peter's voice booming out. 'Looks like something out of a horror movie, doesn't it?'

His mum sat open-mouthed staring into space, her hands

twisting nervously in her lap. It was as if she was frozen in time.

Daphne broke the silence and getting out of the car took a deep breath and said, 'Right we're here and had better take a look. Come on you two, let's get it over with.'

Their mum seemed to come out of her trance as they walked across the drive, the gravel crunching under foot. 'I bet the door creaks when it's opened,' Peter quipped. 'Look at it, it's huge.'

There was a large brass handle set into the wall and as Peter pulled it a clanking sound could be heard. It seemed to resound far in the distance.

'It seems very quiet for a nursing home, Mum,' Daphne muttered. 'Oh, I can hear footsteps.' Each step seemed to echo, gradually becoming louder as someone approached the front door. As the door was pulled open it gave a resounding creak.

Peter looked at Daphne and grimaced. 'Told you so, didn't I!'

A lady dressed in a drab grey and white uniform stood in front of them, her grey hair tucked behind a cap which was perched precariously on her head. She seemed to be eyeing them up and eventually said, ' Ah you must be Mrs Smythe-Cartwright, please do come in. I'm Mrs Collins, deputy head of The Pines. I know you've already spoken to Mrs Phillips.'

The three of them trooped in, and were led into a large waiting room. Huge tapestries hung on the walls along with even older looking oil paintings. You could hardly make out what the pictures depicted they were so dirty. There was an air of neglect about the place, and a smell of stale urine seemed to hang in the air. Old brown, heavy brocade curtains hung at the window – it looked as if they hadn't been washed for years. Fusty, dusty and musty were the words that ran through Daphne's head.

Peter glanced at her and she in turn glanced at her mum who then looked at Peter. They all had a look of desolation on their faces and Peter's mouth hung open in disbelief.

'Now, what we will do Mrs Smythe-Cartwright,' ignoring both Daphne and Peter, 'is this. We'll start with the residents' lounge first. It's just along the hall on the left.' She led them down the hallway and into another large room furnished in a similar fashion to the waiting room. Placed round the wall were various chairs in which the residents were sitting.

It was a sorry sight. Some of them had their heads rolled to one side, their eyes just gazing at the wall. Others were just staring ahead into space with dribble trickling from the corner of their mouths. Someone else sat there constantly twisting the rug that had been placed over her knees, the aged fingers working fast, twisting and pulling while muttering, 'Where are you Bert, where are you?' The look of agitation on the poor woman's face was clear to see.

A hand suddenly grasped Peter on his shoulder, and sharp fingernails dug into his skin. The smell of stale cigarettes filtered into Peter's nostrils as an old man stuck his head next to his face, and yelled, 'Got here then you old sod, did you? Told me you'd be here yesterday, what kept you?'

Peter lurched forward in disgust and a nurse quickly appeared and helped the old man back to his chair. 'There, there Joe, calm down, I'll fetch you a nice cup of tea and then it will be time for a rest.'

'Don't want a rest, don't want a rest,' and he started to wave his arms in the air. 'Leave me alone, leave me bloody well alone. I know you're trying to poison me, I know what you're trying to do.' His voice rose higher as he spoke and spittle flew out of his distorted lips.

'Now don't be silly Joe,' the nurse exclaimed, 'no one's going to hurt you.'

Daphne overheard the nurse muttering to a lady in a white uniform who had suddenly appeared. Before Daphne could count to twenty the woman had returned holding out a plastic pot with two pills in it. 'This ought to calm him down,' she stated in no uncertain terms. 'It will keep the old bugger quiet, he gets on my nerves!'

With a sigh and a shudder the old man burst into tears and started to sob like a baby. 'I don't like it here, I hate it, I want to go home. Oh someone help me, please.'

'I'm sorry Mrs Smythe-Cartwright, I can see it's distressing for you but we do have some patients who have a high degree of dementia. Our staff are very well trained in dealing with the patients you know. Now come along, I'll show you the dining room and then some of the bedrooms.'

As they left the lounge a little old lady shuffled up to Daphne and grabbed her hand. 'Come on luv, help me find Dotty, I can't find her. She's around here somewhere. Help me find her will you? Dotty . . .'

There was a sound of desperation in her voice that made Daphne's heart sink. Snatching her hand away she ran to catch the others up. She was just in time to see them disappear around a corner. There was a sign saying 'Dining Room' on the wall. In stark contrast to the rest of the house it was actually a pleasant room, with views out over rolling lawns. The tables had bright cloths and were obviously laid for the next meal. It was distinctly different compared to what the other rooms had been like. Daphne wondered if it was ever used.

'Now up these stairs, that's right. There is a lift for patients, but they are always supervised of course. Ah, here we are. This is one of the single rooms, but there are a few twin rooms too. Some of our patients like to share and we do get couples from time to time.'

Peter shivered as he stood in the room. It was as though he could feel the history of the building imprinted into its very fabric. It made him feel uneasy.

Although the home had tried to mask the smells that came with uncontrollable bodily functions, the odours still managed to linger. As they moved along a dim corridor and were shown several of the other rooms Daphne nudged Peter. 'Let's get out of here, I don't like it at all, and look, Mum's face is quite puce.'

They made their excuses, grabbed hold of their mum's arm, and eventually were able to escape the persistent mutterings of Mrs Collins who was now well launched into a hard-sell monologue.

In the end Peter was quite blunt and told her that the home was totally unsuitable for their grandfather, and that there was no point in discussing the matter further.

They all gave a sigh of relief once outside and felt the gloomy feeling that had descended on them start to slip away.

Daphne put her arm around her mum, known affectionately to her grandfather as Pips (her real name being Philippa), and gave her a warm squeeze. 'Definitely not, eh Mum?'

'Definitely not,' she exclaimed and her eyes filled with tears.

One by one they got into the car, a sinking feeling in their stomachs and perturbed looks on their faces. Daphne sighed and with a shaky voice asked, 'Where next?'

'Well,' said her mum, who was now sniffing into her handkerchief, 'Why don't we drive over to Compton Dell and see Compton Court. I suggest that if we don't like the look of it from the outside, or we have an uneasy feeling about it, we don't go in.'

'I agree, Mum,' Peter exclaimed.

Daphne nodded her head slowly in agreement, her voice coming out no more than a whisper, 'Compton Court it is then.'

Peter scratched his head and turning to look at his mum said, 'Do you two remember that time Grandfather took us up on Mallow Common? He was convinced he knew the way, wasn't he?

'We did get there eventually, although a thirty-minute journey ended up being two hours. It was a glorious day. Blue skies overhead and fluffy white clouds drifting on a soft, gentle breeze. The hedgerows were bursting with new life. Everything was so fresh and green. A feeling of anticipation hung in the air as nature worked its magic and sprang to life. It all smelt so new. It was almost as if you could feel the changes taking place.'

Peter smiled, looked thoughtful and continued reminiscing. 'I laughed so much when Grandfather told us he'd found the ideal spot to cross the stream. Then when he'd stepped off the bank, he found himself up to his knees in water. After yelling out in surprise he wobbled and swayed, then fell full length into the stream. The family of ducks, who had been happily lazing on the other bank fled in terror as he flapped his arms and legs around, splashing us too. We all ended up soaking wet, but felt ecstatically happy. It was such fun.'

Their mother's face beamed and she broke into laughter. 'He told us it was his old war wound that had caused him to stumble. But we realised later it was the start of his illness.' A silence hung in the air as they all dealt with their own inner thoughts and feelings.

'Right!' Peter spoke loudly breaking their reverie. 'We're here.' They all turned their heads to look at a low, sprawling building. The garden that was spread out on all sides looked wild and untamed. The house itself had a sad look to it; dull, drab and uninviting.

Three disgruntled voices exclaimed in unison, 'NO, NO, NO!'

Without hesitating Daphne took out her mobile and telephoned the home. She told them they wouldn't be keeping their appointment. The matron explained that the home was now to be sold for re-development and they couldn't have taken a new patient anyway.

When she related the news to the others, Peter became really angry, his voice rising to a level not normally heard. 'Bloody cheek, I say, letting us think it was a possible choice.' His anger was getting the better of him.

'Oh, shut up Peter,' first Daphne and then his mum yelled. 'We didn't like the place anyway, so it doesn't really matter does it?'

He sank into the corner of his seat, that little schoolboy expression spread across his face.

'Hang on you two, I've got a text message, best check who it is. What? Oh.' Daphne's face looked crestfallen. She turned to her mum and spoke with a tremulous voice. 'It's from the hospital, Mum; they want us to go there as soon as possible.'

Peter turned the car around, screeching the tyres in his haste and headed off in the direction of St Thomas's. A tangible silence filled the car as each dealt with their reactions to the message.

Daphne was aware there were tears filling her mum's eyes. She leant forward from the back seat, and placed her hand on her shoulder, squeezing it gently in the hope she would draw some comfort from it.

'It'll be all right, Mum, don't worry, perhaps they've come up with an alternative solution. You never know.' However, Daphne's words didn't really ring true and her mum didn't really take any comfort from them.

The car screeched to a halt, and three really anxious people alighted. Although St Thomas's was a modern state-of-the-art hospital, it did nothing to alleviate their fears.

'Oh Mum, what's happened?' and Dahpne burst into tears and stared blankly down at the tarmac.

'For Christ's sake Daffers stop your snivelling and pull yourself together,' Peter's voice bellowed out and seemed to rush around the car park and then slam back, resounding in her ears making her jump.

They all dashed through the hospital door, colliding together and ending up causing such a commotion that the security guard glared menacingly. In a deep voice he told them to be quiet, which drew unwelcome attention to them and once they had collected themselves together they crept down the corridor to 'West Wing', unsure of what lay ahead.

Sister McArthy was coming out of her office and she beckoned to Pips to join her. Pips' face looked harassed and her brow was etched with lines.

It seemed an eternity while Peter and Daphne waited in the corridor. They couldn't talk and to be honest neither of them knew what to say. So they just fidgeted around like two young children waiting to be called into the headmaster's office for a showdown.

The door slowly opened and out walked their mother, a determined look on her face. 'Come on you two, it seems your grandfather has become very lucid and is demanding we take him home. Apparently he's ranting and raving about the barn. Sister told me he keeps repeating, "It's there! Just got to get it."'

As they walked onto the ward there was no mistaking the loud voice.

'Help get me out of here. Damn hospital. Who do they think they are, trussing me up like some Christmas turkey? Let me out. I say, let me out.' His voice echoed around the ward and there were startled looks on the other patients' faces.

'Crikey Daffers, what the hell is going on?' Ignoring her

disgruntled reaction, Peter rushed over to his grandfather and tried to placate the irksome elderly gentleman.

'Dad it's Pips.' Their mother spoke firmly and took hold of his wrinkled hand. 'It's all right, we're all here, calm down.'

'Oh Pips is it really you? I need to get to the barn. You've got to take me.' He was by now standing at the side of the bed, his posture straight as if he was on the parade ground.

Peter grabbed his clothes out of the bedside locker while Daphne drew the curtains around the bed. 'It's all right, Mum, I'll dress him.'

Pips and her astounded daughter rushed off to organise a wheelchair.

'I can't believe it, Mum, what's going on? He's been so ill and then all of a sudden he's talking coherently and able to stand and bellow out orders. It doesn't make sense,' and Daphne tugged at her hair nervously, something she'd always done as a child when she was anxious.

Placing a comforting arm around her daughter Pips spoke gently, 'We just have to go along with it, that's what's best. Otherwise he'll become even more agitated.'

'Here you are Mrs Smythe-Cartwright,' and a young, blonde-haired nurse pushed a wheelchair over to them. I've found an old blanket and sister says she doesn't mind you borrowing it. It's a little unusual to allow a patient out this way, but we can't really stop him. He's determined to have his own way. But you will have to sign this release paper before you go. There are strict rules and regulations around that sort of thing you know.'

Through all the mayhem of the next ten minutes somehow everything was sorted and organised. Once they were seated in the car, although it was a little crushed now with the additional passenger, things seemed to become calmer. There was orderliness about everything. 'It must be Grandfather's influence,' Peter mused.

There were no mishaps on the journey home and eventually with much deliberation they pushed and shoved the old wheelchair through the barn doors. The rusty hinges creaked and groaned as the doors were slowly forced back revealing a dark, dank area. It smelt damp and fusty and it took some breaths to adjust to the atmosphere. Cobwebs hung everywhere and restless hands flailed around casting the insistent webbing from hair and faces.

'Over there, that's it, there.' Grandfather's voice sounded clear but was soon lost in the void of the near-empty barn. No one had been in it for years. When Peter and Daphne were young they had played for hours amongst the hay. Imaginary games: secret agents hiding from special forces, runaway children being sought by indignant parents, wizards and witches making spells from concoctions of magical potions. Oh they were happy days.

'Come on, push,' Grandfather's voice startled them. 'Over there, that's it, in that corner.'

'But there's nothing there, Grandfather,' Peter and Daphne chorused.

'Oh yes there is,' and he pointed his walking stick, a determined look on his old face.

'Come on Pips,' he bellowed at their mother.

'Christ, Peter, how can a man who appeared to be losing the plot suddenly become so strong and lucid?' Daphne scratched her head and a confused look was clear to see on the young face.

'I don't know Daphne, there must be a reason for it. Let's just go along with him.'

Daphne grinned at him, a puzzled frown appearing as Grandfather spoke. 'That's it here, no a bit further to the right, stop!' Their grandfather swung his stick in the air and then pointed to the ground.

'There's nothing but old hay and layers of dirt,' Pips exclaimed.

'Don't be so stupid girl, I'm telling you it's here. Clear the floor, get a spade, a broom, anything, come on move.'

Pips looked at her children and exclaimed, 'Well then, jump to it!' and they all began searching for something to clear the floor with.

'Will this do, Mum?' And Peter held part of an old rake up.

'Yes, anything to appease him,' his disgruntled mother barked back.

The rake moved backwards and forwards grabbing at the remnants of bygone days that lay scattered on the barn floor. It was with some trepidation that Peter continued clearing the ground. A musty smell filled the air as the old debris was disturbed.

'Look, there it is,' and the eager eyes of their grandfather fastened on some old floorboards that could now be seen.

'Of course,' Pips exclaimed. 'This used to be an old inspection pit. I thought it had been filled in years ago. Quick, try and lever the boards up. Hurry up, for goodness' sake. It's all right, Dad, we're doing the best we can, don't fret so.'

Peter and Daphne worked together. It became a lot easier when Pips handed them an old spade she'd spotted propped by the barn door.

'Go on, that's it.'

Daphne's laboured breath spat out the words 'Oh, Oh ...' and two startled bodies fell back in a heap as one of the boards at last gave way and flew up with a crack.

More hands scrabbled to remove the remaining ones, but all that could be seen was a dark empty space. A look of disappointment appeared on their faces and just as they were thinking it was a hopeless situation Peter jumped down into the hole.

'What the hell do you think you're doing Peter?' Daphne's voice, tinged with fear, rang out.

'He bloody well jabbed his walking stick into my back. I didn't have a choice! If I hadn't jumped I would have toppled face first into the damn hole!'

Daphne turned and looked at her grandfather who was grinning from ear to ear.

'Never stood any messing from the lads in the forces, don't see why I should now.' And he banged his old stick against the side of his wheelchair. What a clatter it made too!

'Right, young man, feel around for a metal ring, come on, get to it!'

Peter raised his hands in the air in a gesture of frustration and with a look of 'Well I haven't got much choice have I?' He bent down and started feeling around in the damp earth.

'Gawd, this is horrible.' Black sticky soil and goodness knows what else stuck to his fingers. It stank too. 'Yuck this is just gross. Wait, ah, ah ..., I can feel something.' And two inquisitive faces looked down on him, eyes wide, mouths open.

'Get out of the way, I can't see a thing with you gawking at me. Get a torch or something. Quick, get a move on.'

Peter now sounded like his grandfather and within minutes two torches were hurriedly thrust down to him.

'Steady on, don't be in such a hurry,' Peter bellowed as he nearly dropped them.

'Oh you're impossible,' Daphne spat out. 'You tell us to be quick and then you're blasted well moaning. No pleasing some people is there?' And she stamped her foot impatiently.

The beam of the torch was now focused on a rusty metal ring. Peter jabbed and poked to clear the soil and free the rusty old box from its hiding place.

'It's here grandfather, I've got it, you were right all along.'

'Of course I was lad, I haven't lost my marbles you know. Anyone would think I'd been ill.'

Three faces with perplexed looks on them turned to look at the person they all so loved. Then with a few coughs and throat-clearing diversionary tactics the box was released from its hiding place and lay on an upturned crate alongside the wheelchair.

An old tired voice spoke with determination. 'The answer to all your problems lies in there, so stop your worrying.'

And before their startled eyes it was as though a door closed in his mind, a cloud descended and his body slumped into the corner of the wheelchair.

'I'm old you know, old and tired,' and large salty tears trickled out of the corners of his eyes and made damp patches on the hospital blanket.

'Oh Dad,' and in between her own sobs Pips hugged her father as best she could and told him she loved him.

Daphne held his hand while her shoulders shook with her own emotional outburst and her own words of love poured out.

And Peter, his frustration and anger now dispersed, moved his mother gently out of the way, bent, and with misted eyes thanked him for all the good years they'd shared and kissed him tenderly on his cheek. 'You're a good 'un Grandfather and I love you.'

There was a visible tiredness now that took over the old man; his lucidity had slipped away. Slumped in his chair he looked so frail.

Gently the three people who so cherished and loved him, took him back to the safety of the hospital and stayed to comfort him until he fell asleep and looked at peace.

Later that evening they sat around the old kitchen table, the warmth from the huge log fire filling the cosy room.

Oranges, yellows and reds threaded together inside the flames creating dancing shadows on the walls. Sparks crackled and spat out as the timber burnt and settled, the once resplendent tree that had stood grandly in the garden now in its final process as it became no more than ash.

'Well, let's open it, shall we, Mum?' and Daphne patted her arm.

'Right Peter, you've a selection of tools there that might do the trick, so get to work,' and his mum looked at him expectantly.

As he picked up the hammer and file chosen for the job excitement mounted. After a lot of prising and banging the box fell open and a bundle of papers wrapped in a waterproof covering dropped onto the table.

Their mother of course was the one to open the bundle and there was a look of wonder on her face which engendered a feeling of excitement in Peter and Daphne.

'What is it, Mum? Come on, tell us!' The eager voices of her children reached through to her at last.

'They're bonds, stocks and shares. I never knew they existed. I had no idea. This means, that, that ...'

Daphne finished what her mother had been trying to say, 'That Grandfather can now be cared for at home. Whatever needs to be done for him, can now be done.'

Their mother turned and looked at them and with a cracked voice said, 'It's a miracle isn't it?' and through the tears, the smiles shone and three very happy people hugged each other and laughter once more filled the kitchen.

A Poem or Two

The Moment Paused

The moment paused
And I drew breath
Knowing yesterday had slipped away
And here was today that
Would soon be that yesterday too
That all our days
Become yesterdays
And all our days are tomorrows
And all our days are todays
No one moment of our day can be reclaimed
It is gone, lost forever
In the sea of time
Just a memory
A bubble floating out there
That will never float back again

Walk Tall

Woman
I held your hand and kissed your cheek
Knowing the pain you felt went deep
I imagined tears that should fall from your eyes
Understanding that a man sometimes cries

Man
Why shouldn't a man cry if he need?
Pent-up emotions must somehow be freed
The hurt at times felt is no less
And crying would take away the stress

When a heart's heavy and weighed down with grief
Can't a man let it out, not keep it beneath?
Walk tall my man you're strong and brave
Society decrees your pride you should save

Walk tall they say? When my heart has broken
The words within I wish I had spoken
For deep inside I feel like a child

But I mustn't let go, no I must smile
But alas, down the side of my cheeks came
Like a never-ending torrent of rain
Tear after tear rushing forth from my eyes
The floodgates had opened, damn my pride!

**A humourous story we had to write
So hear all about our Gav's plight**

102

Our Gav

The taxi pulled up outside the corner café having rumbled along the cobbled one-way street. More wear on the tyres, the grumpy taxi driver thought. I hate these tiny Cornish streets, don't know why I've stayed here for thirty-odd years. He sighed and scratched his now balding head. 'Right you are Missus, this is it,' and he turned to stare at the run-down café with its dilapidated blue awning hanging precariously in tatters, the odd chairs and cheap plastic tables stacked inside against the dirty windows. 'Needs a bit of a clean up, doesn't it?' he muttered and went on to address the issue of the fare.

'Come on you! Get a move on,' Debs's voice screeched out from the back of the taxi. 'Move your arse!'

She scrambled out dragging her teenage son with her. Thick as two short planks he was. He was just a pest to her, an unnecessary item in life she had to cope with. How I got landed with him I'll never know. But then she did know. Somehow she couldn't help taking it out on him. A pang of guilt hit her like a brick. But, shrugging her ample shoulders, she carried on in the same old vein.

'Right, our Gav, you get the cases out of the boot and I'll pay the driver.'

As she delved into the pocket of her well-fitting denim jacket, which was teamed up with clinging leopardskin patterned leggings, her other hand grabbed at her ample bosoms and tried to grapple them back into the cups of her fine netted black bra. Knew I shouldn't have had that boob job, they've gone all saggy and baggy.

The taxi driver eyed her with contempt. Her cheap sickly perfume had given him a headache on the short distance from Netherby station. He scowled at her.

With pouting bright red lips she voiced. 'Here you are mate, thanks very much. Oh, and keep the change.'

The twenty pence tip looked lost in the palm of his sweaty hand. Mean cow, he thought. Wouldn't want to give her one, you would suffocate amongst those mounds of flabby flesh. Crikes, looks like she needs hammocks to keep those big tits in place. They looked like over-ripe watermelons.

He revved the engine and with the car's exhaust rattling as it edged its way along the cobbles back to the main road he laughed our loud. She'd be a right 'novelty ride' for sure.

Debs took her flashy, jewel-encrusted cigarette lighter from her handbag and lit up. Deeply inhaling the smoke, she sighed.

'Looks a real dump for sure.' Her voice sounded forced. 'Well, better make the best of a bad job I suppose. Boy, it does look like a real dive though.'

Glancing at Gav she frowned. Just look at him: dark, lank, greasy hair and those pimples. How could I have produced something like that!

Her voice full of scorn she shouted, 'Get a bloody move on will you.'

She fumbled for the key, fishing around in the depths of her Armani handbag, a copy of course, bought in Turkey. Her bright red nails grasped the bundle of keys; the small pink fluffy dice dangled and swayed as she put the key in the lock. The old door creaked open. A smell of stale air hit her and she was glad of the slight breeze that filtered in through the open door.

'God, what a dump.' Her eyes roamed around the untidy dirty interior of the coffee shop. She caught sight of the *book* the solicitor had promised to leave for her, it contained all the contacts she needed that would help get the business up and running.

'Get them cases upstairs, Gav, get to it lad. And take those trunks up too. At least they've arrived and we can unpack and make it a bit homely. Get a move on will you.'

Gav shrugged his bony shoulders. Who does she think I am – a bloody skivvy? He knew his mum didn't like him. It wasn't his fault. She'd gotten herself pregnant at fifteen. Sometimes he'd wished he'd been adopted. At least he would have felt wanted. Selfish, that's what she was – actually not just selfish but a slag too. He'd lost count of the numerous men that had crept into their run-down council house at night. He used to stick earplugs in to shut out the sound of the grunts and groans that came from her bedroom.

'Find us a pair of scissors will you, I need to cut the bloody plastic ties on these boxes. Don't want to wreck my nails. Cost me thirty pounds to get them done.'

Gav stuck his tongue out and put his fingers up in a rude gesture. One of these days, she'll pay, you mark my word.

Huffing and puffing he ferreted in the kitchen drawers. At last he found what he was looking for and careered down the stairs. 'Don't know how she's going to cut with these, they look pretty blunt to me,' he muttered.

Not being used to the stairs he hit the bend full on and felt himself slipping and then wobbling. Trying to regain his balance he can only describe what happened next as a . . . he couldn't quite put it into words.

Falling forward with flailing arms and legs he screamed out with fear. 'Aggh . . . 'ucking hell.'

As he fell he saw his mother's back at the bottom of the stairs, her peroxide, bleached hair, brittle and fluffy, standing out from her bowed head.

She never knew what hit her. Turning, startled by Gav's screaming and the clumping as he fell, she stood frozen to the spot. There was no escape for her.

As they collided, the scissors, their blades gleaming as they caught the light from the now well-lit café, made contact with his mother's flesh.

Her eyes stared in disbelief and her mouth fell open. A strangulated scream gurgled up from her throat.

They lay in a heap, legs, arms and flesh in contact with each other. Prising himself off his mother's sprawled body he scrambled up and looked down at her.

'Bloody hell.' He could see the scissors were standing up out of her left boob. Blood was oozing from the wound and a strange looking liquid seeped slowly out of the mound of flesh. 'Bloody hell.' His mouth fell open and he rubbed his eyes in disbelief at what he was seeing.

Debs crawled to a chair clutching the well-embedded scissors, which were firmly fixed in the breast implant.

'Fucking hell. Get an ambulance.' Her voice rose to a pitch that made Gav want to put his hands over his ears. 'Dial 999, get an ambulance for Christ's sake!'

As Gav grappled for his mother's mobile in her well-filled handbag he stared at her. As his fingers hastily keyed in the 999 she slumped to the side and slid to the floor and lay quite still.

He shook as words spun around his head. Gee, she's dead and I've killed her. I said, I'd make her pay, and I've done it. I didn't mean . . .

Tears spilled out of his eyes and when the paramedics

arrived he was slumped on one of the packing cases staring into space.

A year later Gav was sitting in the park. The wooden bench he had chosen was the one that looked across the bay. Love hearts and initials were carved deep into the wood. He laughed when he remembered that day he had fallen and stabbed his mum. That fateful day that had brought about change.

His hair was cut in a modern style and shone in the sun. He had put on some weight and it suited him well. The spots had gone and he'd grown himself a stylish beard. He felt good. Sea air really suited him.

He looked at the lone woman walking along the cliff path, her brown hair cut in a stylish bob really suited her lightly tanned face. The light coating of make-up she wore and the delicate layer of pale lipstick adding a touch of colour to her lips really enhanced her features. Her black trousers and stylish tee shirt suited her and fitted well over her trim figure. She looked calm and at ease with herself.

Oh, there was old Bob hobbling along on his 'daily constitutional', as he called it.

Poor old Mrs Flyn looked harassed, she was always rushing around. Same old clothes whatever the weather. Tweed skirt and jacket with a roll-necked sweater. Gav never knew how she could cope with the heat. Fancy wearing those clothes on such a warm day. He laughed at the stupid miniature poodle of hers, what a name – Gabby. She had to race to keep up with her mistress. They made many heads turn out of curiosity. But that was life – the misfits, as he liked to call them.

Lots of holidaymakers were milling around. Chatter, laughter and happy squeals filled the air.

The coffee shop was thriving now. His uncle and aunt had

moved down and between the three of them they'd got it up and running. It was popular with not just the holidaymakers but the locals too. Life felt good.

'Ah, there you are, Gav,' and the 'lone woman' sat down beside her son.

Turning, she smiled at him. She patted his arm and they looked at each other.

He loved these meetings with his mum; they'd gradually got to know each other over the past months since the accident.

'You know Gav, this last year has been hard but the accident and my breakdown helped me realise a lot of things. I am glad we're friends now, you are a really special son.'

A lump rose in Gav's throat and with difficulty he said, 'It's OK mum, I understand now.'

Both of them contented and at ease with each other, they turned and gazed out over the bay and watched the boats bobbing gracefully on the water.

Well, here we are nearing the end of this journey. I am amazed that my work is written here, to be shared and enjoyed.

So, the theme this evening: 'strange happenings'. Until my pen touches the page I have no idea what will appear before me. It always surprises me, thrills and excites me. There is great satisfaction in it.

My courage through the Journey of the Writer has stayed steady. The group has helped along my motivation. The encouragement has led me to believe in myself. We never know what we can achieve until we try.

So go forth my friends, take that first step ... you never know where it will lead you.

Grandpa's Bench

'Oh, this darn bench ain't like it used to be.'

Those blooming layabouts from the village had been hacking at the slats again with their flick knives. He scratched his ear in a contemplative way and muttered, 'In my days the local bobby would have boxed them round their ears, they wouldn't have dared do it again. I don't know what the world is coming to!'

Restlessly he shifted his tired, aching body. His rheumatism had been really playing up the last few weeks. The old joints seemed to set quickly now and when he tried to move they clicked and pained until suddenly they jolted into movement.

'If I'd known I was going to live this long, I would have looked after meself a bit better I suppose. I know, Em, I keep drifting back into me old West Country dialect. You tried hard to get me to speak proper like, but without you around to keep me on me toes, I don't do very well, Em.'

He hadn't realised he'd been muttering aloud and he sensed the spittle running from the corner of his mouth. He stretched his arm up and rubbed the sleeve of his old, rough overcoat against his face, wiping away the spittle that was now running down his chin. Although ripped and dirty, it did the trick nicely, and with his mouth dry once more, he allowed himself to think back to that warm, spring day when he'd been taken by Granny Day to the local park.

Granny Day were a right caution. She had grizzled hair that was pulled back into a bun on the back of her head. There was a crusty wart on her cheek that wagged around when she talked, and boy could she talk; she never stopped. She had a bit of a short fuse too. He'd felt the back of her hand once or twice when he'd been cheeky, but he loved her to bits. She had a laugh that used to rise from deep inside her chest followed by a deep cackling sound, which reverberated up her throat, and out of her tiny, rosebud mouth. He hated being scolded by her, but it never lasted for long. She'd look at him, a whimsical expression on her face. Then throwing her arms open wide would pull him to her, crushing him against her ample bosom in an enormous embrace. She was always quick to forgive and reassure him that all was well.

He remembered the old wishing well, all covered in moss and creeper, that was hidden away behind the old café. The excitement he'd felt had made a shiver run down his back, like an explorer finding an ancient ruin, and in his little mind he had conjured up pictures of buried treasure lying at the bottom of the well, just waiting to be found.

'Mmm, I wonder if the well is still there. It's all of seventy-five years ago now.'

A puzzled look appeared on his face. Where had all the years gone to?

Granny had given him a ha'pence to drop in the well and he had wished in all his childish innocence for a big bag of sticky treacle toffee, but he never got any.

'I ain't got no teeth now to have that stuff,' he chuckled. 'I have a job to sup me scrumpy let alone chew on anything.'

He slipped his wrinkled hand into the inside pocket of his overcoat, ferreted around and, finding what he was looking for, drew it out. It always had the same effect and he sat there with a tear slowly rolling down his craggy cheek. It left a clean trail through the grime on his face, but he wasn't even aware of the layers of dirt that had built up on his skin over the past months.

'Old, that's me, old!'

He sighed and looked at the photo of Em. She sure was a pretty young thing. Her hair was the colour of ripened corn and her eyes blue like newly opened cornflowers. He'd loved the way she smiled, it was like the sun coming out, and when she laughed her eyes lit up.

He remembered with tenderness the nights at the Palais when they had danced for hours until their feet had ached and throbbed.

'Eh love, they were good days weren't they? Real good days.'

She'd been dead nigh on twenty years now, but it had seemed forever. He walked over to the cracked headstone in the corner of the churchyard. The grave was clear of the vegetation that had grown over many or most of the other graves. It was part of his day to tweak out a weed or two and make it look tidy like. Em had kept a tidy house. He knew she would like a tidy grave.

'Em, you shouldn't have left me on my own, you really shouldn't have. I have been right lonely you know. You spoiled me rotten all them years and when you were gone I didn't have a clue how to look after myself. A fine pickle you left me in woman! You certainly did! Hopefully you are up there looking down with a little pity for your old Bert. Ay, love?'

The sound of the church clock striking six startled him and he realised the night air was creeping into his old bones. 'Blooming body of mine just ain't no good any more. If I were an old Austin Seven I'd have been sent to the scrap yard by now. Clapped out, that's what I am.'

He clutched the photo, stared at the gravestone and another tear slowly pushed its way down the side of his face. The clean track made by the second tear joined the first and they etched their way along his scrawny flesh. Lately he'd got so muddled in his head and couldn't always remember what he was doing. Sometimes night became day and day became night.

His mind wandered back in time again. He'd been 'right 'ansome' in those days. Lots of the Palais girls had had their eye on him. But no, only Em had caught his eye. He remembered how he could fit his hands round her trim waist. Oh those were the days.

He turned and stumbled back to the bench. 'I suppose it won't help to spend another night out here in the churchyard, best be making my way back.'

Placing one old foot in front of the other he dragged his tired body along the twisting gravel path and pushed open the rickety wooden gate that led into Smithy's Lane.

His stomach rumbled and he realised how hungry he was.

As he stumbled on his way he started talking aloud. 'There's a nice bit of cold mutton waiting in the larder and if I cut the mould off the bread it'll fill me up till I go down to the Roosters tonight.'

Bert had a liking for scrumpy: a few jars in the evening helped him sleep through the long, cold, dark nights.

It was quite dark now, and the hedges loomed at him out of the darkening night, rearing up like monsters from the deep. A shiver went up his spine as a gust of wind suddenly blew him nearly off his feet.

'Where did that come from?' he murmured.

Another gust tugged at his overcoat and he leant into the

wind and trudged on. A huge gnarled branch on the old oak tree was swaying erratically. It creaked and groaned, as the wind became more forceful, twisting and turning as though someone had hold of it and were trying to wrench it from the trunk, its dried-up, crispy brown leaves blowing around in the wind like whirling dervishes as they were wrenched free from the branch.

'Just like me that tree, old, wizened and breaking up.'

The branch gave one more groan and with a loud cracking sound crashed down onto the road pinning Bert to the ground.

'Ah, HELP! HELP!'

But no sound came from his mouth. His heart was beating fast and he could feel a trickle of something warm running into his eye. It smelt sweet, but he couldn't brush it away as his arm was twisted under him and seemed to be at a strange angle; the other was pinned firmly under the huge branch. There was an eerie silence all around. It felt as though time was standing still.

He felt a sharp pain in his stomach that was beginning to get worse. Catching his breath, he peered from his other eye and he saw a silhouetted figure walking slowly towards him surrounded by a swirling white mist. He recognised her at once.

'Em, that you Em? You're back, you're back, oh Em.'

The tears flowed fast and he saw Em reaching out her hands, a smile on her face and love shining from her eyes.

Bert gasped loudly, a perplexed look on his face.

'It's crazy what you start thinking when you're dying, I promised old Jack a game of crib at the Roosters tonight. Well I'll just have to break my promise, haven't got any choice really have I?'

He saw Em smiling and then, with one last shuddering sigh, he let go of his old worn-out body and reached out to her. She took his hands, and like two ghostly shadowy figures they both drifted away into the night.

The rector found Bert the next day on his way to the church. He didn't see him at first. He was so well hidden by the massive branch and after all he hadn't been expecting to see a body lying there in the road. It gave him a real shock. He was as white as a sheet as he raced to the inn screaming wildly and banged loudly on the door. His fists were clenched tightly as time and time again he rained blows on the door trying to rouse the landlord from his bed.

'HEEEEELP.'

As he continued screaming the sound of his voice trailed off into the cold morning air. All sense of reverent composure had disappeared by now.

The landlord threw the door wide open with a jerk and barked, 'What the hell's going on?' When he saw the rector he stopped dead in his tracks.

'Come quick, come quick, poor old Bert's trapped under a huge branch that's been wrenched off that big old oak tree,' the rector gasped, his chest heaving with the effort of speaking.

There was a real good send-off for Bert after he'd been laid to rest with his beloved Em. The inn had never had so many people through its door. There were right shenanigans that night, I can tell you.

'My dad's happy now Fred, isn't he?' a tired voice was heard to say to the rector. A largish man with a head of unruly blond hair and the most amazing blue eyes was leaning against the bar with a pint of scrumpy in his hand.

'I'm sure he is Peter. I'm sure they have cider vats in heaven too.'

Peter laughed and looked at the rector, saying, 'If that's the case then I haven't anything to worry about.' And went on happily supping his cider.

When given the topic of 'an estate agent', the scope was endless. I've never worked out how stories formulate themselves. I just allow it to happen.

An aside to this is the question of editing. The reading, re-reading and the re-reading. The story can lose its impetus. I find it best to edit part of it and then put it away and edit some more later. It is just great when someone else reads out your written word, it has brought tears to my eyes. 'Did I write that?' Wow!

So my closing story brings to an end (at least in this book) my first amazing achievement of being a writer and if you're reading this in print, my success at being published.

Follow your dreams, make them reality and celebrate achieving them.

The Salesman's Smile

Ryan's red sports car roared round the country lanes, wheels screeching, as he drove like a maniac on his way to Clifton Grange. The grange, an old crumbling manor house, which stood on the outskirts of Grinton, had been on the market for a long time. No one really wanted to spend the money on it to bring it up to date. He had the chance now for a really big commission and so wanted to create a good impression.

Perspiration stood out in beads on his forehead, and he could feel the damp on his shirt under his armpits as his stress levels mounted and his fear grew.

Being an estate agent wasn't easy and he had not expected to be rushing off into the depths of the Surrey countryside to appease some stuck-up actress called Sheila Pearson on a Sunday evening. What a name anyway, Sheila for goodness sake. You would think she could think of something better.

He knew he was going to be late and with his foot pushing that little bit harder on the accelerator he swung into the driveway sending gravel spraying in all directions.

'Blast, she's here before me,' he muttered to himself. With a deep intake of breath and putting on his best salesman's smile he drew up beside Ms Pearson's Alfa Romeo.

She looked none too pleased, and with a haughty gesture

stared him straight in the eyes and verbally slated him. 'Where the bloody hell have you been? Well?'

He choked and then coughed loudly to cover up his nervousness. Pulling himself up to his fullest height he said, 'I do apologise Ms Pearson, but there was a herd of cows on the road. I had to wait at least fifteen minutes for the farmer to move them out of the way.'

'Huh, oh yeah!' reeled out from her rose-red, pouting lips. 'Yeah, sure.'

He felt the heat of the sun beating down from the clear blue sky burning into the back of his neck and sweat began to trickle down under his collar. Damn it, he thought, why do angry, pushy females always make me so bloody nervous.

Easing himself from the car he went to stand in front of her.

She glowered at him and a look of hatred spread across her face. 'I can understand you getting angry at having to wait so long, but isn't this a little over the top?' Ryan stated sheepishly. He knew that stupid cheesy grin of his was showing on his face but he could do nothing to stop it. Inside he was quivering like a little school kid. All command of the situation had eluded him by now.

'Ryan Taylor isn't it?' Ms Pearson sneered.

'Yeah, that's me. Why, is it a problem?' He knew he was imitating her sneer and he could see a deep flame of annoyance showing in her eyes.

She walked a little nearer and spat out her next sentence. 'Ryan Taylor who used to go out with Megan Roberts?'

'Yeah, but how do you know that?' he exclaimed. He faced her square on and repeated the question. 'How do you know that?' there was a quizzical sound to his voice.

'Well, she was my younger sister. When you dumped her for that slut of a blonde bimbo she came to me. She told me what a nasty, two-timing jerk you were.'

'I- I- I ...' he started to speak.

She interrupted him, anger burning in her eyes. She stamped her foot and shouted, 'Shut up, shut up. I hate you. You're nothing but a jumped-up little upstart. I hate you, do you hear me, I HATE YOU!

'You weren't the one who found her crumpled body were you? You weren't the one who touched her and felt the coldness from her dead body seep into your hand! You aren't the one who can't forget seeing those wide open, staring eyes. No, it was me! Yes, I found her!'

Her hand crept eagerly and purposefully into her designer-labelled shoulder bag. Without him realising what was happening she'd raised the gun, and pulled the trigger. With a look of utter astonishment on his face he fell backwards onto the gravelled drive with a resounding thud, his salesman's smile wiped from his face in one swift, skilful blast.

She stood there with a look of pure satisfaction on her face, her arm hanging relaxed by her side, and the gun dangling from her fingertips.

Suddenly a deep, male voice boomed out, 'CUT. That's a take!'

Epilogue

Well here we are, the journey has been completed – or maybe not! You may have cried a little, laughed a lot. Perhaps the stories have been thought-provoking and your slant on life and death is now different. I think food for thought is a very positive thing and I do hope that we have journeyed well together through my experience of The Writer.

Thank you for your time, and I wish you a safe journey through life. May it be rich in many ways and joy and happiness mark your path.

Bless you.

In appreciation.

Mary Earle

Lightning Source UK Ltd.
Milton Keynes UK
UKOW052326191011

180612UK00001B/6/P